MARX AT THE ARCADE

MARX AT THE ARCADE

CONSOLES, CONTROLLERS, AND CLASS STRUGGLE

JAMIE WOODCOCK

Haymarket Books
Chicago, Illinois

Published in 2019 by
Haymarket Books
P.O. Box 180165
Chicago, IL 60618
773-583-7884
www.haymarketbooks.org
info@haymarketbooks.org

ISBN: 978-1-60846-866-9

Distributed to the trade in the US through Consortium Book Sales
and Distribution (www.cbsd.com) and internationally through Ingram
Publisher Services International (www.ingramcontent.com).

This book was published with the generous support of Lannan
Foundation and Wallace Action Fund.

Special discounts are available for bulk purchases by organizations
and institutions. Please call 773-583-7884 or email
info@haymarketbooks.org for more information.

Cover design by Rachel Cohen.
Text design by Jamie Kerry.

Printed in Canada by union labor.

Library of Congress Cataloging-in-Publication data is available.

10 9 8 7 6 5 4 3 2 1

CONTENTS

AUTHOR'S NOTE

The ideas for this book began as an article in the *Journal of Gaming and Virtual Worlds*.[1] It has been rewritten, expanded, and developed into the present form here.

ACKNOWLEDGMENTS

I would like to start by thanking John McDonald at Haymarket for encouraging me to turn my ideas about Marxism and videogames into a book. That conversation over the stall at the New York Historical Materialism conference was the start of a great collaboration, and I would also like to thank Nisha Bolsey and the rest of the team at Haymarket for their support, as well as Brian Baughan for copy editing the book.

This book could not have been written without the support of Lydia Hughes—not only her encouragement throughout the entire process, convincing me that the book was worth doing, and finishing, but also her help with the "crunch" points during the process. The irony is not missed that I crunched while writing about how bad such a practice is at work.

I would like to thank my parents for their support, as well as for letting me play videogames—who would have thought that those experiences would turn into a book later? My dad encouraged me and introduced me to my first videogames. Many of these came through his friend Jim, so thanks for all those floppy disks.

The book owes a huge debt to my comrade Solvi Goard, who not only played videogames with me but also talked through—at length—many of the ideas that I've put forward here.

Working with Mike Cook and Mark Johnson proved an invaluable experience for understanding how videogames are actually made, with thanks to both for their (often very patient) explanations. Thanks also to Mike for letting me test out some of the ideas (well, at least the slide of Marx's face on a robot) at the hugely inspiring PROCJAM conference.

An earlier version of the argument in this book was published in a special issue of the *Journal of Gaming and Virtual Worlds*, and I would like to thank both Lars and Graeme for all their feedback. I was also greatly inspired by Nick Dyer-Witheford and Greig de Peuter's *Games of Empire*, a book I returned to regularly while writing. It has also been great talking with both Nick and Greig during trips to Canada, as well as Daniel Joseph, whose work too has been really useful.

The politics of this book have been deeply shaped by my editorial comrades Lydia Hughes, Seth Wheeler, Callum Cant, Achille Marotta, and Wendy Liu at *Notes from Below*. The special issue on technology by Wendy and Marijam (as well as *Left Left Up*) helped me to think through many of the issues for the book. Sai Englert provided invaluable pun support (I'm sorry none of them made it into the title!).

Finally, I would like to thank Game Workers Unite (GWU) and particularly its UK branch. Sitting in your meetings and talking through what organizing should look like today has been hugely inspiring (and also a bit difficult to write about—in a good way—as things are moving so fast!). I would like to thank Dec, Beck, Karn, and Austin (among many others). You have all shown that there is clearly no such thing as unorganizable workers. This book is dedicated to all of you.

INTRODUCTION

Popular culture is one of the sites where this struggle for and against a culture of the powerful is engaged: it is also the stake to be won or lost in that struggle. It is the arena of consent and resistance. It is partly where hegemony arises, and where it is secured. It is not a sphere where socialism, a socialist culture—already fully formed—might be simply "expressed." But it is one of the places where socialism might be constituted. That is why "popular culture" matters. Otherwise, to tell you the truth, I don't give a damn about it.

—Stuart Hall, "Notes on Deconstructing 'the Popular'"

One of my earliest memories of videogames is sitting in front of a computer, trying to figure out how to work the MS-DOS operating system. A friend of my dad's gave him games, loaded onto floppy disks, to pass along to me. Sometimes they came in plain paper packaging, other times in larger cardboard boxes, filled with paper manuals and other ephemera. I would write down the instructions for playing different games on Post-it notes, which became scattered around the screen. I remember thinking that the games required some expertise, that you had to learn to play them.

Those early games, pixelated and colorful, were a route into another world for me. I directed *Lemmings*, using different commands to try and stop any from falling off cliffs. I ventured out from the crashed spaceship of *Commander Keen*, eagerly investigating the game's world. I also, for reasons I never quite understood, explored the Fantasy World of that anthropomorphized egg with a hat, *Dizzy*. Then there were the videogames like the platformer *Duke Nukem*, in which I shot my way through levels. All of these games were passed along by someone who programmed computers for a living.

I was taught to play *Tetris* on a Nintendo Game Boy while sitting on the staircase of a family friend's home. Another friend taught me to play console games, introducing me to *Sonic, Mario*, and others. I remember sitting on the floor, poring over the paper manuals while *Civilization* installed, wondering whether the installer had crashed or if the loading bar could really take so long. I felt at the time that *Civilization* was not just a game but that it had educational value—another reason for "just one more turn."

My paper manual for *Street Fighter Alpha 2* had all the pages torn out, so I had to try and learn the moves with friends while we battled it out in front of the TV. I built sprawling metropolises in *SimCity*, astonished that I could then fly a helicopter through them in *SimCopter*. *Baldur's Gate* was the closest I ever got to *Dungeons & Dragons*: I would meet with friends to compare notes on how the characters and story developed. Moving on from those games, I explored postapocalyptic wastelands in *Fallout* and played for the evil side in *Dungeon Keeper*.

The first console I ever owned was a PlayStation. I still vividly remember the sound effect and exclamation mark flashing on the screen upon a player being discovered in the stealth game *Metal Gear Solid*, along with the "Snake? Snaaaaake!" at game over, and the shock of the boss fight that broke the fourth wall, making it seem like the TV channel had accidently changed. At the time broadband internet first became widely available, I built my own PC. That need for expertise was there again, brought on by the fear that static electricity would damage the components, along with the ongoing debate with my friends about the best way to apply thermal paste to a CPU. The first online videogame I played was *Counter-Strike* version 1.4, and I have played that series on and off since. I played *World of Warcraft* on that custom PC too.

Many of these videogames from my childhood have aged badly, while others have been transformed as the game series evolved. I have no doubt forgotten many that I played, but I can place these older games within periods of my life, which brings back much-broader memories. Videogames have been with me almost my entire life, and the continuing pace of their development is dizzying. Over this time, videogames have also become a form of mass culture. Last year nearly 70 percent of Americans played videogames, while the global industry generated revenues of $108.4 billion.[1] Videogames no longer feel like a pursuit that requires niche expertise to access—they are everywhere now.

Now that I am older, videogames are something I have to make time for—whether unwinding after work or carving out the time to dive into a new title. I have a Steam collection with more un-played games than I would care to admit, but I still do find the time to play videogames and talk about them. In a way, the process of researching for and writing *Marx at the Arcade* was also an excuse to play some more videogames. It also provided the opportunity to combine videogames with another of my interests: Marxism.

As I think back to those earlier times, who would have thought that twenty years later Karl Marx would actually have relevance to the world of videogames? It is a rare combination that might seem like quite a jump to conceive. But then again, the Old Moor did recently make his digital debut in *Assassin's Creed Syndicate*.

Syndicate, part of the long-running Ubisoft series *Assassin's Creed* and released in 2015, is set in London in 1868. The plot covers convoluted time travel, battles between Assassins and the Knights Templar, bizarre technology, and everything else that players have come to love and expect throughout the series. The main character, Desmond Miles, is trapped within a sinister corporation and made to relive the genetic memories of his ancestors. This provides the backdrop for the player to visit key moments of history, including the Third Crusade, the French Revolution, and the golden age of piracy, among others.

Despite this complicated plot, the game also provides the backdrop for this book. It highlights some of the key dynamics of contemporary videogames and draws attention to themes that will be explored throughout the book as well as providing an example of Marx in an actual game, in a way that deftly introduces him into the analysis. Upon loading *Assassin's Creed Syndicate*, a statement flashes on the screen: "Inspired by historical events and characters, this work of fiction was designed, developed, and produced by a multicultural team of various beliefs, sexual orientations and gender identities." Unsurprisingly, nothing more is said about how workers at Ubisoft made the game. There are no details about how many people were involved, what the work was like, or any disagreements in the process. This gives way to a title screen decorated with turning cogs and indeterminate pieces of metal machinery in motion, with steam drifting over the screen. This is an *Assassin's Creed* set after the Industrial Revolution, in a London filled with factories, dense housing, smokestacks, and railway tracks.

The game revolves around Desmond's assassin ancestors, the twins Jacob and Evie Frye, who are trying to regain London from Templar control and find some sort of artifact. The twins are armed with hidden wrist blades for stabbing people, can free-run up and down buildings, and have grappling hooks for soaring through the air. With these abilities, they make the city their dangerous playground. Their focus is the chief villain, Crawford Starrick, a Templar who is responsible for the current state of London. As one character describes him, "There is no aspect of society he does not control. No industry that escapes his grim touch." In the first mission, the player takes control of Jacob after breaking into a factory. He watches as a child is crushed, screaming in pain. Rupert Ferris, "the industrialist," complains, "How long does he intend to go on like this? He's disrupting the other workers. Shut his trap and get the machine fixed! And send me some laudanum for my head." Jacob replies, out of earshot,

"Coming right up." The player can then free-run across the factory to try to reach Ferris, but will find the door locked. After engaging in some good old-fashioned sabotage of the factory, Jacob can then be directed to drop from the rafters to "air assassinate" Ferris with those hidden blades.

From the killing of Ferris, the story develops into a series of core missions, which involve taking over London boroughs, and many, many side missions. After causing some trouble, Starrick gives the following monologue:

> Gentlemen! This tea was brought to me from India by a ship, then up from the harbor to a factory, where it was packaged and ferried by carriage to my door, unpacked in the larder and brought upstairs to me. All by men and women who work for me. Who are indebted to me, Crawford Starrick, for their jobs, their time, the very lives they lead. They will work in my factories, and so too shall their children. And you come to me with talk of this Jacob Frye? This insignificant blemish who calls himself Assassin? You disrespect the very city that works day and night so that we may drink this. This miracle. This tea.

As I played through this stage of the game, it brought to mind all the different workers and processes that must have come together across the world to allow the *player* to enjoy "this miracle." The videogame, like the cup of tea, requires complex global supply chains and different kinds of labor to ensure the final object can be consumed by the player. Uncovering these supply chains today will take more than just studying the lines of an evil monologue.

The first encounter with Karl Marx in *Assassin's Creed Syndicate* takes place in the packed Whitechapel train station, somewhere I used to pass through daily in modern, real-life London. Moving through the crowds, Marx can be spotted arguing with a policeman. In his German accent he shouts: "You cannot frighten me! I insist on being heard!" Once the player reaches Marx, a pop-up notes that the player can start the mission titled "Karl Marx Memories: Cat and Mouse" and that they will need to "help Marx avoid the London Police." In a cutscene (a short expository clip in a videogame), the twins approach Marx, who introduces himself: "Much like you, I am an activist of sorts." He explains that the twins "have done more for London's citizens lately than any endeavor has accomplished in a decade. But those citizens were already well provided for. I challenge you both to help those who *really* need your assistance. The working people." Before Jacob can say anything, Evie replies, "An interesting challenge. We accept." Marx explains that he is "organizing a discreet meeting with some like-minded friends to discuss trades unions." The player is directed to "follow Marx." A good start to the mission!

The first mission involves the twins protecting Marx by killing spies. The next encounter starts with Marx standing outside a factory. A pop-up announces the mission: "Find proof that a factory is abusing its work force." Marx explains:

> Corruption reigns here, I am sure of it. The number of people injured by their machinery cannot be calculated, and yet the company continues to prosper. They must be stopped for the sake of the poor workers they abuse. If only we had some form of proof. There must be records of the accidents somewhere inside which would surely prove their malfeasance. I should think you would need to find the foreman, but how you'd convince him to give you the reports . . . Perhaps . . . if they think the factory is on fire, you might bluff your way past.

The player is directed to "find and ignite the cotton bales" along with the optional "air assassinate a guard." The player can then break into the factory, jumping in through a window. While the machinery whirls around them, the player sets fire to cotton bales, and the factory fills with smoke. The next step is hijacking a fire truck, bringing it back to the factory. The foreman comes out thinking they are being saved, but the player's character replies to them, "Saved, are you daft? What about the reports? Your masters won't be happy." The foreman, followed by the player, goes to retrieve the reports. Once back outside the factory, the player picks the foreman's pocket, securing the reports for Marx.

Videogames, it may be no surprise to hear, often take quite a lot of artistic license with historical details. Marx did not employ twin assassins to kill spies with hidden gauntlet blades. Nor did he convince them to break into factories and steal reports. The historical account is, at least as far as we know, much less exciting. The reality is that Marx drew on the publicly available factory inspectors' reports. He would later also experiment with the use of surveys as method of "workers' inquiry" to interrogate and understand workers' conditions.[2] This moment of inquiry in *Assassin's Creed*, albeit far removed from Marx's actual methods, is one favorable to being turned outward and used to examine the industry that produced it. It suggests a way to unpack the type of relationships that Starrick identifies in his tea monologue, and it poses a critical question: Where does a game like *Assassin's Creed* come from? What does the game's creation entail—from the workers who developed it to the supply chains that make it playable at home, easily appearing as a modern "miracle," much like Starrick's tea. Instead of convincing assassins to break into the workplaces of the videogame industry, this book will explore what we can learn when applying Marx's methods of inquiry in the present day.

Back in *Assassin's Creed*, there are two subsequent missions about an attempted bombing, which Marx asks the player to prevent. Marx is presented as a pacifist, while the bomber is branded an anarchist. The final mission, "Vox Populi," involves meeting Marx at a pub in Southwark. After the assassins knock out a number of people who try to disrupt the meeting, a full-on brawl erupts, with shots fired. After saving Marx, the assassins are asked: "I don't suppose you'd formally join the workers' party." Neither assassin takes up the offer. The rewards flash up—"£1100+150, XP 850+150" and a "colors: wine"—which means from now on the characters are virtually richer and more experienced, and can also choose red clothes. The assassins may not have joined the communists (although this option is not left to the player), but they can now at least look the part (which, of course, I immediately did while playing the game).

We know, of course, that Marx had nothing to say of videogames, given they did not exist at the time (though he was a chess player, and there is even a record of a game he played after he finished writing *Capital*).[3] Similar to the Frye twins' mission, in this book I will "follow" Marx, taking a journey through the world of videogames. Part 1 is a discussion of how videogames are made, in which I cover the history of play and videogames, analyze the videogames industry, and focus on the work of videogames, as well as how workers are organizing today. In part 2, I discuss the play of videogames. This includes thinking about how to analyze culture, and looking at key genres of videogames, the role of politics, and what has happened to online play. The conclusion will argue that Marxists should be interested in videogames (despite the fact many have ignored them) and that videogame players can benefit from adopting a Marxist analysis.

Videogames are a terrain of cultural struggle, shaped by work, capitalism, and ideas about society. Through the pages that follow, I will draw out the struggle and resistance that has marked videogames from the start, thinking about what that means for today.

PART I

MAKING VIDEOGAMES

A HISTORY OF
VIDEOGAMES AND PLAY

Before getting into how videogames are being made and played, the first question that needs to be answered is, what actually is a videogame? No doubt, you have a sense of what a videogame is, but what defines a videogame can be quite hard to pin down. One hint of this challenge is the fact that there is still disagreement about exactly what term to use. Even though I have ducked this dilemma in both the title and subtitle of the book, I use the term "videogame" throughout. It seemed the sensible choice. When I was growing up, "videogames" was the broader term; "computer games" would refer to those on computers, whereas separating the term in two—like "board game"—never seemed appropriate. So there is some controversy over terminology. More than merely a cause for academic debate, the terminology says something interesting about videogames and is thus worth exploring a little further.

To illustrate this (fairly minor) controversy, I decided to take to Twitter—a social media platform upon which controversy is indeed a well-worn theme—to pose a question. In a polling tweet, I asked, "Academic writing question: which term do you prefer?," offering the options "videogames," "video games," "video-games," or "something else."[1] As one of my colleagues quickly replied: "You just threw a rock at a hornet nest, Jamie!" While some participated only by voting, a few people also commented. One commenter noted that "at least we can all agree that one option is total nonsense." One commenter closer to my own view explained they "like that 'videogames' implies that they are their own cultural item—while 'video games' feels like they're just an extension of other screen media." Out of a total of 167 votes, the vote broke down as follows: 48 percent for "video games," 44 percent for "videogames," .05 percent for "something else," and .03 percent for "video-games." Apart from this, it was clear that some people would prefer—from an academic standpoint—to describe them as "digital games." For example, one person noted that they "use digital games unless it seems like the audience wouldn't understand that term, then video games (the one correct answer)." Another struggled with this issue in their PhD dissertation, trying "as much as possible to say 'digital games' just to be as ecumenical as possible."

This was perhaps not the most scientific approach to settling on what term to use, but the reason to explore this is to show that the terminology regarding games (as well as the boundaries of what constitutes them) is contested. It also shows that this is a topic people care about. For example, if this were a book about Marxism and film, it would be much clearer what to call the subject. In part, this is because whatever we choose to call them, videogames come in a wide variety of forms. As Bill Kunkel, who was arguably one of the first journalists to ever cover videogames and founded the first magazine dedicated to them, has argued:

> ["Videogames"] doesn't make sense grammatically, but that's how the industry spelled it and I always felt it reflected the unique nature of the medium. We spelled it that way in '78 and I never stopped. What I did not realize was that, over the years, a schism developed over the spelling. I didn't realize how deeply people felt about it until I suggested that we would adopt that one-word spelling.[2]

The reason this spelling difference is worth drawing out is that it also reflects the bigger challenge of defining what a videogame is, which is also the subject of some controversy. For example, in one of the experiments by the radical independent game developer Molleindustria, a browser-based application randomly generates a definition of what a game is. This pokes fun at the tensions, highlighting the difficulty in where to draw the line, what to include, and what to leave out. My favorite randomly generated definition (so far) is the following:

> game /gām/ n. (pl. -games) a dynamic medium that involves a structured conflict toward a trivial goal.[3]

This nicely summarizes one way we could look at videogames. Games are "dynamic," as the player interacts with them; they involve a "structured conflict" in that they are rule-bound systems in which the player tries to achieve something within the game: a "trivial goal." However, this example does not cover the range of videogames that have been created.

A more technical definition we could use is "a *game* which we *play* thanks to an *audiovisual apparatus* and which can be based on a *story*."[4] This definition, provided by Nicolas Esposito, means we are looking at a format in which the player interacts and plays with a game, which might have a narrative. The interaction happens via an "audiovisual apparatus"—a computer, console and television, smartphone, tablet, et cetera—that differentiates it from other kinds of games. The key difference is that unlike the "non-electronic precursors"—board games and so on—these kinds of games "add automation and complexity—they can uphold and calculate game rules on their own, thereby allowing for richer game worlds; this also lets them keep pace."[5] This recognizes another important aspect of videogames: that "gameplay is the component . . . that is found in no other art form: interactivity."[6] This kind of interactivity represents a break from other forms of art or culture, along with what has become the mass reach of videogames. However, despite the novelty of videogames, play and games have a long history.

PLAY AND GAMES

When we turn on a videogame, our intention is to play. Play is an interesting and difficult concept to try and understand under capitalism. Play, by its very nature, is an unproductive activity. In the wake of neoliberalism, we are constantly told about the virtues of work—not only while we are doing it, but needing to constantly prepare and train for it too. Play appears to run against this. It is often viewed as wasted time that could be better spent developing our own "human capital" or some other bleak management-speak. However, despite this emphasis on productivity through "capitalist realism,"[7] play is still viewed as important in the context of human development.

Because play has a recognized role in childhood, it is often diminished, relegated to a developmental life phase, not as a serious activity. As Johan Huizinga argued, "Play is more than a mere physiological phenomenon or a psychological reflex ... it is a *significant* function—that is to say, there is some sense to it. ... All play means something."[8] The difficulty is unpacking *what* play means in the context of videogames. Is it a way to get rid of excess energies, to prepare or train for more serious activities, to relax and recover, or some combination of all of these? In this vein, play only makes sense in relation to work and is not valued in and of itself. It also means that play is often in the background, despite the large part it plays in all our lives. Huizinga continues:

> Such at least is the way in which play presents itself to us in the first instance: as an intermezzo, an *interlude* in our daily lives. As a regularly recurring relaxation, however, it becomes the accompaniment, the complement, in fact an integral part of life in general. It adorns life, amplifies it and is to that extent a necessity both for the individual—as a life function—and for society by reason of the meaning it contains, its significance, its expressive value, its spiritual and social associations, in short, as a culture function.[9]

There is a recognition here of the importance of play in how we recover and prepare ourselves as workers outside of work.[10]

However, play is not simply about this. Huizinga also goes further, stressing the importance of play to culture. These hard-to-measure aspects of play mean that it can take on quite-romantic connotations. As Huizinga summarizes:

> We might call . . . a free activity standing quite consciously outside "ordinary" life as being "not serious," but at the same time absorbing the player intensely and utterly. It is an activity connected with no material interest, and no profit can be gained by it. It proceeds within its own proper boundaries of time and space according to fixed rules and in an orderly manner. It promotes the formation of social groupings which tend to surround themselves with secrecy and to stress their difference from the common world by disguise or other means.[11]

We could quite easily apply this understanding to videogames. Think of the times you have been absorbed by a videogame, something that does not bring any material benefits outside of the game. It feels like for that moment of play you have been sucked into another world, with the demands and stress of the outside world suspended.

This kind of romantic idea has led some to discuss play in games as taking place within a "magic circle."[12] From this perspective, games can be understood on their own terms. We can then just explore how people play within those "magic" boundaries. For example, it has been argued that these imaginary boundaries "can be considered a shield of sorts, protecting the fantasy world from the outside world."[13] Katie Salen and Eric Zimmerman have gone as far as arguing that "there is in fact something genuinely magical that happens when a game begins."[14]

While this sounds really exciting, there is nothing actually "magical" at all about playing games. Instead of setting up an imaginary barrier around play, we need to understand how both play and games are rooted within the economic and social relations of society. This is something that Nick Dyer-Witheford and Greig de Peuter have argued in their excellent book *Games of Empire* (a text that I will return to throughout this chapter and beyond):

Games have always served empire: from Cicero's claim that gladiatorial sports cultivated the martial virtues that Rome required to the Duke of Wellington's apocryphal assertion that the Battle of Waterloo was won on the playing fields of Eton or the Prussian general staff's Kriegspiel rehearsals of their World War I Schlieffen Plan. But games have also turned against empire, in ways ranging from the bloodbath of Spartacus's revolt to the gentler revenges of the West Indian cricketers defeating their colonial British rulers.[15]

That Huizinga did not look at the world this way is hardly surprising, as he was a conservative medieval historian. However, he does raise some interesting ideas about play.

We can also look to Roger Caillois's writings, which critique Huizinga, to think about play under capitalism. Caillois argues that play "creates no wealth or goods, thus differing from work or art." In the process, he argues, "nothing has been harvested or manufactured, no masterpiece has been created, no capital has accrued. Play is an occasion of pure waste: waste of time, energy, ingenuity, skill, and often money for the purchase of gambling equipment or eventually to pay for the establishment."[16] Caillois's definition of play is particularly useful if we apply it to videogames. He argues, first, that play is a "free" choice; otherwise it loses its nonwork qualities. Second, it is "separate" from other parts of life, limited in terms of space and time, defined before the activity starts. Third, the outcome is "uncertain," meaning the player must take initiative as the results are not fixed beforehand. Fourth, it is "unproductive," not creating anything in the process. Fifth, it is "governed by rules" that create new conventions and ways of doing things while also suspending the regulation of everyday life. Sixth, it is "make-believe," meaning it is different to, and set against, real life.[17] When play is defined by these six aspects, it is often structured by games.

We can clearly see each of these qualities with videogames. We make a "free" choice to play them, usually within the "separate" environment of the computer or console; we do not know how the play will go in advance, as videogames are "uncertain"

(even if we are really good at the game); the activity is "unproductive" in the capitalist sense; the videogame contains complex
"rules," even if many are hidden from the player; and they are
"make-believe" in varying ways. If play encompasses spontaneous and hard-to-capture aspects (what Caillois identifies with the
Greek word *paidia*), then games introduce structured activities
with explicit rules (*ludus*), as well as the elements of competition
(*agôn*), chance (*alea*), simulation (*mimesis*), and vertigo (*ilinx*, referring not to the nausea-inducing physical experience but to the
simulation of high speeds or of a reckless rampage).[18] Becoming
broadly familiar with each of these qualities will help us make
sense of different types of games later.

Caillois was also a surrealist who saw great political potential in avant-garde art. As such, his arguments for politics and
games started from the idea that "for the player to voluntarily be
liberated by play/game as a means for a free society, the game
has to project a belief system that is beyond a known reality."
In the process, he reproduces part of the magic circle as "the
game has to remain separate from reality."[19] We can take up these
insights from Caillois by reading him through Marx, in which
case the concept of play would also begin from a separation, not
from reality, but "from everyday work, separate from the production tools owned not by the worker but by the employer,
the capitalist."[20] The process of play can therefore be a "means
for the worker to cease being a worker, for a limited time, and
to become, in a surrealist sense, 'something else' than a slave in
the bounds of the capitalist."[21] This resonates much more with
videogame play. Coming home after work to play videogames
provides that escape for millions of workers every day. For a moment, each is no longer a worker, but free to explore new worlds
outside the drudgery of capitalism.

Videogames provide a space of experimentation, of discovery,
but also recovery from capitalist work. In a way, Marshall McLuhan makes a similar claim, arguing that "art and games enable
us to stand aside from the material pressure of routine and convention, observing and questioning. Games as popular art forms

offer to all an immediate means of participation in the full life of a society, such as no single role of job can offer to any man."[22] It is clear that games have historically played important social roles. As McLuhan notes, "The games of a people reveal a great deal about them."[23] Therefore, we next should consider how videogames developed over time.

A HISTORY OF VIDEOGAMES

The history of videogames may not be as long as that of play, but it is still complex. Some might be surprised at the length of videogame history, as well as the forces that have shaped them over time. It is a story of different sides: of hackers and corporate control, radicals and the military, free software and proprietary code, the material and immaterial, resistance and capture, and escape from work and entry into new careers, among others. It is also the story of the growth of a capitalist videogames industry that takes place over half a century. Those early videogames that I discussed above are far from being the first, and many since have been lost or almost forgotten. Videogames are no longer new; nor is the industry.

To start at the very beginning, the Strong National Museum of Play in New York claims that the very first videogame was a custom-built computer in 1940, the Nimatron. It played a version of the game *Nim*, in which players must avoid picking up the last matchstick. (On the Nimatron, this meant turning off lights that represented the remaining matchsticks.) The computer was built into a cabinet that looked a little like the arcade machines that would come later, and it was featured only briefly at the World's Fair. In 1947, a patent was filed for a "cathode ray tube amusement device," which, although it does not sound that fun, connected to an oscilloscope display for players to shoot a gun at.[24] In 1950, Claude Shannon published a paper about designing a computer program to play chess. He noted that "although perhaps of no practical importance, the question is of theoretical interest, and it is hoped that a satisfactory solution of this problem will act as a wedge in attacking other problems of a similar nature and of greater significance."[25] In the same year, Shannon and Alan Turing separately created programs that could play chess. However, this did not lead to the widespread play of chess videogames right away. These were not videogames in the modern sense of the term. They were early curiosities and experiments, technical demonstrations rather than something fun to play around with.

The technological basis for videogames was laid by the US military. As Dyer-Witheford and de Peuter have argued, "They originated in the U.S. military-industrial complex, the nuclear-armed core of capital's global domination, to which they remain umbilically connected."[26] The military-industrial complex was enlisting the "first draft of immaterial labor, the highly educated techno-scientific personnel recruited to prepare, directly or indirectly, for nuclear war with the Soviet Union." This preparation meant establishing academic research centers with military funding and developing "the massive defense-contracting system, in which the giants of U.S. corporate power, including information and telecommunication companies," including IBM, "prepared for doomsday."[27] The expertise put to work in academic, military, and corporate laboratories was also applied to early games. In 1952, A. S. Douglas created a noughts and crosses game (more commonly known as "tic-tac-toe" in the US) on Cambridge's EDSAC computer for research. Two years later, at the Los Alamos laboratory (infamous for the Manhattan Project and the atomic bomb), programmers in their spare time developed the first blackjack game for the IBM 701.[28]

These early videogame links to the military-industrial complex were further solidified in 1955 with the introduction of the military war game *Hutspiel*, which simulated a war between NATO and the Soviet Union, represented, respectively, by blue and red characters. The similarities between these simulations and later videogames was riffed on in the 1983 film *WarGames*, in which Matthew Broderick's character hacks into a military supercomputer. On finding a simulation called "Global Thermonuclear War" installed on the system, he believes it is a game and begins to play as the Soviet Union. In actuality, he is playing against a program that controls the real missile-launch control centers, which also do not realize this is a simulation. The situation almost reaches nuclear war (which also nearly came to pass later in real life), but Broderick's character is able to use tic-tac-toe to show that only no-win scenarios are available in nuclear war.

In 1956, on national television Arthur Samuel demonstrated a checkers program for the IBM 701, which six years later would defeat a master checkers player. In 1957 Alex Bernstein wrote a complete chess program on the IBM 704, which at this stage could calculate four moves ahead. One year later, William Higinbotham demonstrated a tennis game that played an analog computer and oscilloscope, but it was dismantled after two years and mostly forgotten about. It did, however, lay the groundwork for *Pong*. Students at MIT created a basic game called *Mouse in the Maze* on the TX-0 computer. The original version featured a mouse seeking cheese through a player-drawn maze, but this was later updated to a mouse hunting out martinis to drink. In 1960, John Burgeson, off sick from work at IBM, designed a baseball simulation. Returning to work in 1961, he ran the statistics-heavy program on an IBM 1620. The same year, Raytheon developed a simulation of the Cold War for the US military. The simulation was too complex for most users, so an alternative analog version was developed.[29]

In 1962, two major events in the early history of videogames took place. The first followed the Cuban Missile Crisis, which saw the launch of the computer war game *STAGE* (Simulation of Total Atomic Global Exchange) by the US Department of Defense. Rather than ending in mutually assured destruction, the simulation predicted that the United States would defeat the Soviet Union in a thermonuclear war.[30] Unfortunately, unlike in *WarGames*, there is no record of the simulation playing tic-tac-toe to show otherwise (luckily, this has never been tested in practice; otherwise the history of videogames—and the rest of the world—would be much shorter.)

Within the "military-academic-industrial complex" that emerged, computer systems became "integral to this closed world, a crucial means to calculate the options of nuclear strategy, to think the unthinkable."[31] Also around this time, an MIT student named Steve Russell invented the game *Spacewar!* The game represented an important break, showing that "simulations could also be a diversion from working on mass death if they were cut loose from serious application, enjoyed for their technical 'sweetness' and oddity without instrumental purpose, transformed into play."[32]

Unlike the previous demonstrations of potential uses for computers, of working through the practicalities of nuclear war, *Spacewar!* was a game designed to be *played*. These kinds of escapes became possible, in the words of Dyer-Witheford and de Peuter, "because the military allowed its immaterial workers a lot of latitude." Unlike the user of the Raytheon military simulations, these immaterial workers understood how to program these computers. Therefore, "transgressing standard procedures, fooling around with computers, was at least tolerated because that was the way to discover new uses and options. Such transgressions included making games."[33] *Spacewar!* spread across the military ARPANET (a predecessor to the internet), where it was played but also added to and modified in various ways.[34]

Dyer-Witheford and de Peuter identify not one but two "red scares" that occurred with the intersection of videogames and the military-industrial complex. The first was the external competition between the US and Soviet Russia. The second was internal—the combination of the countercultures of hacking and the New Left. This emerged with the opposition to the Vietnam War, along with campus demonstrations and the broader social upheaval of 1968.[35] The later scare could be seen in the distributed and collaborative nature of *Spacewar!* It came from the early culture of "computer-science 'freaks'" that stood in opposition to institutions and the military. The students at MIT came together in the Tech Model Railroad Club, finding ways to get access to the computers for what they began to call "hacking."[36] It was not driven by the desire to make money. John Kemeny, who was also involved in the military-industrial complex as part of the Manhattan Project, represented another example of this kind of early ethos of videogames. He created the BASIC programming language and a time-share system for computers at Dartmouth College. The former made it easier for students to write games, while the latter provided access to the hardware to test and play them. This led to many more games being written and experimented with, under the idea that everyone could be a programmer.[37]

While Higinbotham and Russell were contenders for inventor of the videogame, it was Ralph Baer who had the first commercial success. In 1966, Baer developed the idea of playing videogames on a television. This was a wild idea at the time, but it laid the basis for future consoles. A year later, he developed the "Brown Box," a not very exciting name for a prototype that played tennis and other games. Baer filed a patent in 1968, and four years later Magnavox released the Odyssey, a videogame system designed to be played in the home, based on his designs.[38] Alongside this conventional success, there continued to be a proliferation of games along the hacker lines. For example, in 1970, the rules for the *Game of Life* (also known as *Life*) were published in *Scientific American*.[39] In this game, the player sets an initial state, which is a configuration of cells, then through the application of series of rules, they observe how it evolves. These rules were then implemented by hackers on their computers, providing free access to the game. A year later, students at Carleton College in Northfield, Minnesota, created *The Oregon Trail*. The simulation game was designed to be played on a single teletype machine, but was later distributed nationally in the US.[40]

This all changed with the release of *Pong*. The table tennis arcade game was launched by Atari in 1972. A test version was installed in Andy Capp's Tavern in Sunnyvale, California. It was so popular with players that it broke after too many quarters were put into the machine. This eagerness to spend money on videogames led to the development of *Home Pong* three years later. However, it failed to be picked up by toy shops and instead was sold in the Sears Roebuck sporting goods department as if it were actually a version of tennis.[41] Videogames were struggling to find their place as they began to become popular, and the challenge of how to market *Home Pong* serves as proof that the problem of definition was present then as it is today. Despite this, Atari became a hugely successful company, "a technological innovator at the heart of a burgeoning Silicon Valley computer culture," with a sense of experimentation that was later captured in the AMC television series *Halt and Catch Fire*.[42] Atari was able to channel the "refusal of work" that came out of the student movements of 1968. This refusal of work saw young workers rejecting the jobs their parents' generation had and refusing to work on capital's terms. Companies like Atari promised "play as work" as an alternative to the restrictive conditions of industrial or office-based Fordism. This was an early innovation of the "work hard, play hard" workplace culture that would become so influential in Silicon Valley. However, the company later sold out to the decidedly non–anti-work Warner Communications.[43]

Around the same time, in 1973, David Ahl published *101 BASIC Computer Games*, which included code for the games *Chomp*, a two-player strategy game; *Hexapawn*, a smaller pawn-only chess game; *Hamurabi*, a text-based resource management game; *Nim*, discussed earlier; and *Super Star Trek*, a very popular text-based game where the player commands the USS *Enterprise*. The book would go on to sell a million copies, with tens of millions of home computers able to run the games by the 1980s.[44] The first-person perspective was introduced in 1974 with *Maze War*, a game with basic wire-frame graphics. Don Woods's version of the text-based game *Adventure*, released in 1976, took inspiration from *Dungeons & Dragons* and laid the basis for future role-playing games. All of these examples were, in a way, a continuation of the DIY ethic and hacker traditions of early videogames.

My dad was a student in 1974 and played his first videogame on a 12-bit Digital Equipment PDP-8. It was a simple golf game that had to be bootstrapped into the machine by manually inputting instructions on the front panel, after which the game's results were outputted onto a teleprinter and paper. Inputting the instructions entailed selecting a particular kind of golf club and indicating how hard it should be swung; then the program printed the trajectory of the golf ball as a parabola of period marks. This required the reversal of the linefeed so that the paper was swallowed into the teleprinter as the ball rose up the parabola. Once the ball had reached the highest it would go, the linefeed resumed its proper direction and the ball came down the parabola to earth and hopefully into the hole. He described it as a "completely addictive game."

The year after, he wrote his first game for a Modular One minicomputer. The computer was meant to be used for teaching, and he was supposed to be in this case writing a calendar program for a class assessment. Instead he wrote a lunar landing game in the GEORGINA operating system's macro job-control language (a specific kind of software language that was not meant to serve this gaming function). The game was visually represented on a Newbury visual display unit that had luminous green ASCII characters on a black background (like those terminals found in the contemporary *Fallout* games). It was inspired by an earlier game on a Texas Instruments scientific calculator and similar to *Lunar Lander*, released by Atari in 1979. The game involved bringing a lunar landing module down from orbit and onto the surface by controlling the engine burn. Success was twofold: the lower the speed at touchdown on the moon, the better, but the player also needed to have enough fuel left to take off again. The game itself was also a successful use of a computer that was not designed for this sort thing, an escape from classwork.

In another sign of that push and pull between hackers and corporations, official and unofficial (with the odds in the corporations' favor), Atari launched the Video Computer System in the US in 1977, later renamed the Atari 2600. This console, featuring a joystick and games on proprietary cartridges, signaled an important step toward the formation of a capitalist videogame industry. The console would go on to sell 30 million units.[45] A year later, the seminal *Space Invaders* was launched in Japan. It became so popular that it caused a shortage of 100-yen coins as they were poured into arcade machines. Videogames had become so popular they were not only showing how much profit could be made, but even affecting the circulation of currency! In the same year, *Space Invaders* flooded into the US on sixty thousand arcade machines.

Around the same time, Rob Trubshaw and Richard Bartle created the multi-user dungeon (or MUD), a text-based adventure. Again, like the earlier hackers, they made it in their spare time, using the computer labs at the University of Essex in the evening. Although he did not work with a military mainframe, Bartle used computers owned by British Petroleum. As Bartle explained, "In order to say sorry for filling the air with toxic fumes they let the local schools use their computer."[46] This early online multiplayer game allowed users to simultaneously log in and embark on *Dungeons & Dragons*–style quests. To do so, they had to hack the computer, by "using an area of memory they weren't supposed to be writing to."[47] Bartle and Trubshaw never sought copyright for the videogame, instead distributing it and encouraging other modified versions. This precursor to online games, which would prove to be incredibly profitable, was made with a very different intention. For Bartle, the "MUD was a political statement, we made a world where people could go and shed what was holding them back."[48]

Atari launched its most successful game, *Asteroids*, in 1979. Around $1 billion of quarters were put into the arcade machines in only a year. In Japan, Namco launched *Pac-Man* in 1980, which brought in around $2 billion.[49] These two arcade cabinet games saw huge numbers of players blasting asteroids and eating pills while avoiding ghosts. If we were to adjust for inflation today, the two games combined brought in around $6 billion. Videogames had clearly become a huge source of profits, paid in the form of quarters while other players waited their turn. These were followed up by characters that would become famous figures in videogame history: Nintendo's *Donkey Kong*, which also featured "Jumpman," who would later be renamed Mario.[50]

After these surging profits, there was a huge crash in 1983. There had been a crisis building in the videogames industry in the US, and it suddenly burst to the fore. The "mix of incompetent management, employee discontent, overproduction, and rampant piracy exploded."[51] The lack of what is now called "digital rights management" led to companies making too many games—what, Daniel Joseph notes, "Marxists would describe as a crisis of overproduction."[52] Atari fell short of projected profits, its stock rapidly fell, and it "abruptly plunged towards bankruptcy. It carried with it the entire industry it had drawn upward on its ascent."[53] This started the first crisis of the videogames industry. While revenues had peaked at around $3.2 billion in 1983, they would fall to only $100 million by 1985, a massive reduction of 97 percent.[54]

In one bizarre moment, this led to Atari burying seven hundred thousand videogame cartridges in the desert in New Mexico. Atari had struck a deal with Warner Communications to make a videogame adaptation of *E.T. the Extra Terrestrial*, which for various reasons had to be made in five weeks to meet the holiday deadline. The resulting videogame was, arguably, the worst ever made. Atari produced 5 million cartridges, and only 1.5 million sold. Its response was then to load up semitrailer trucks with the cartridges, take them to a landfill, and bury them. There are reports that some of these found their way into the hands of local kids who heard about the dumping. After this, a layer of concrete was put over the top of this de facto grave. The story became an urban legend, with the details becoming convoluted over time. It was later revisited by the 2014 documentary *Atari: Game Over*, which charted the excavation of the cartridges and pulled this story back, quite literally, out of the grave.[55]

The burial became a symbol of the videogames industry at the time, with many believing it was no longer viable, because US companies had failed. However, the Japanese videogames industry continued to grow. In the 1980s, this developed to the extent that it became known as the "Japanese video game coup" and "aroused protectionist panic among U.S. capitalists."[56] Instead of competition between the US and Japan, Nintendo was instead challenged by another Japanese company, Sega, which led to them facing off with rival consoles and rival characters—particularly Mario and Sonic. This would later involve Sony, a much larger Japanese company, entering the stage too.[57]

The rise of Japanese videogames is also linked to the military-industrial complex. The irony is that Japan, defeated by the military and nuclear forces of the US, later "excelled in adopting the victors' techno-cultural innovations."[58] The state-led policies in Japan pushed for a postindustrial reconstruction after the Second World War, laying the technical basis for the videogames industry. (This is analogous, in part, to the later experience of South Korea with online gaming.)[59] While the military-industrial complex remained a key part of Japan's development of videogames, so too was there a subversive element drawn into the industry. Deviating from the hacker trend in the US, the Japanese industry "absorbed *manga* talent," practitioners of the Japanese comic format that was, in the process, "changed from an anti- to a pro-establishment medium."[60]

A major success came with Nintendo's launch of the Famicom in Japan in 1983. For other markets it was renamed the Nintendo Entertainment System, or NES, a console that many people have fond memories of—so much so that a contemporary version, the Nintendo Classic Mini Entertainment System, was released to capitalize on that nostalgia. The original console was a huge success, selling just under 62 million units.[61] Nintendo introduced an internal vetting system, meaning only games that the company approved would work on the console. This "approach laid the essential groundwork for platforms today: control through code. With this form of control, Nintendo turned video games from a fad into an industry again."[62]

Nintendo launched *The Legend of Zelda* in 1987, which again became a huge success. A year later a cross-platform game, *John Madden Football*, was launched, the first in what would become a long-running series of sports game franchises. Then in 1989, Nintendo introduced a new kind of videogame hardware with the launch of the portable Game Boy. It sold 64 million units, and with the launch of the Game Boy Color in 1998 (after which the sales numbers were only released as combined figures), then sold a total of just under 120 million units.[63] The original Game Boy came bundled with *Tetris*, the most successful videogame to date with an estimated 170 million sales.[64] The game was originally created by Alexey Pajitnov and was leaked out from the Soviet Union—an ironic success considering it came from the losing side of the Cold War. That same code traveled a far way to the staircase of my family friend's home so that I could play the game.

Another successful puzzle game, *Solitaire*, was bundled with Windows 3.0 on the PC in 1990, leading to millions of new players, many of whom may have never played on consoles. In offices across the world, people found a new outlet for anti-work boredom. While consoles were becoming popular household items, this computer product reached an entirely new audience.

The next stage of the competition between Sega and Nintendo began with the launch of the Mega Drive / Genesis, featuring *Sonic the Hedgehog*. The console went on to sell 30 million units.[65] This was followed by the Super Nintendo Entertainment System (SNES), which sold almost 50 million units.[66] This, too, has been refreshed in the recently released (and now very wordy) Nintendo Classic Mini Super Nintendo Entertainment System, which allows nostalgic players to play classic 16-bit games like *Star Fox 2*, *F-Zero*, *Street Fighter II Turbo*, *Super Mario World*, *Super Mario Kart*, and *The Legend of Zelda: A Link to the Past* on modern flat-screen TVs.

Aside from the consoles, a number of important and genre-defining titles were released on the PC, including Westwood Studios's *Dune II*, the first popular real-time strategy game, and Blizzard's *Warcraft: Orcs & Humans*, which initiated a long-running and hugely influential series.[67] Sony launched the PlayStation, which went on to sell 102 million units,[68] while the Nintendo 64 sold almost 33 million units.[69] The year 1993 saw the launch of the infamous *Mortal Kombat* games, sparking the controversy about violent videogames. Joe Biden, among others, began a crusade against videogames, scapegoating them for violence in US society. (Oddly, the crusade neglected the connection between videogames and the US military-industrial complex that we have discussed, instead focusing on the depiction of violence within them.) The complaints about violence in videogames prompted hearings in the US Senate and the introduction of videogame rating systems. In the same year, *Doom* was launched, popularizing first-person shooting (FPS) games.[70] Then, as the industry began this phase of massive expansion, particularly with consoles and PCs, the role of the military faded into the background.

In 1996, *Tomb Raider* was launched. Featuring the character Lara Croft as its protagonist, the game started a debate on gender in videogames. Dyer-Witheford and de Peuter point out that by the mid-1990s, "80 percent of players were boys and men," which they argue was a result of several factors:

> The military origins of simulations, the monasticism of hacker culture, the bad-boy arcade experience, testosterone niche marketing, developers' hiring of experienced (hence male) players, game capital's risk-averse adherence to proven shooting, sports, fighting, and racing formulae—all combined to form a self-replicating culture whose sexual politics were coded into every Game Boy handheld, every *Duke Nukem* double-entendre, and every booth babe at industry conferences, where women appeared only as imperiled princesses and imperiling vixens, a male head-start program, building and consolidating the gender stratification within immaterial labor.[71]

This shaped the kinds of games that were designed, funded, and made, which in turn affected player demographics, which, again, determined what is considered a popular game. This is a self-reinforcing process that continues today.

Toward the end of the 1990s, two other interesting events took place. The first was the IBM supercomputer program Deep Blue's victory over the world chess champion Garry Kasparov. This was the culmination finally of Shannon's early work on computer programming and chess—which by this point had gone far beyond being "of no practical importance." The second event was Sony Online Entertainment's launch of *EverQuest*. This was an online role-playing game in which hundreds of thousands of players met for cooperative and competitive play. The success of the title signaled the start of widespread online videogame play, a phenomenon that continues to grow today.

The 2000s saw Sega driven out of the console business by the success of Sony's PlayStation 2, which enjoyed incredible success, with an estimated 155 million consoles sold by 2012.[72] Nintendo launched the GameCube, which sold 22 million units. The handheld console market continued to grow, with the Game Boy Advance selling 82 million, and the Nintendo DS selling a vast 154 million units.[73] The Sony rival, the PlayStation Portable, was also a huge success, selling 82 million units.[74] After the dominance of the existing Japanese companies, a US firm reentered the market in 2001. Microsoft, which was clearly not a small competitor, shifted from PCs to launch the Xbox. The console sold 24 million units.[75] Its headline title, *Halo: Combat Evolved*, became a massive success, triggering the development of many FPS games. Four years later, Microsoft launched the Xbox 360, which sold 84 million units.[76] I owned the original Xbox and the 360, both of which bring back a lot of memories. However, despite the vast extent of corporate control at this stage, I also remember a vibrant community of modded (modified) and chipped consoles (which had an extra hardware chip soldered into them) that enabled gamers to play backups (copies of videogames loaded onto another disk—this was only allowed if you owned the original, but people found ways around this). The hacking ethos had definitely not gone away.

The importance of FPS games continued with titles like *Call of Duty*, *BioShock*, and *Borderlands*.[77] Sony's competitor in this generation of consoles, the PlayStation 3, launched in 2006. It reportedly sold just under 84 million, losing out slightly to Microsoft.[78] Nintendo made its bid to compete with the Wii in 2006, which focused on using motion-sensitive controls. The console was targeted at nontraditional gamers and pitched as a more active way of playing games. It sold a huge number of units: 102 million.[79]

The US military once again made an important foray into video-games at this time. Despite having fallen into the background, it developed *America's Army* in 2002 as a recruitment tool. Rather than carrying out the military's previous priority of strategizing for war itself, this product was more about seeing how potential soldiers could be reached through videogames, which signaled how popular games had become. Meanwhile, simulation games, like *The Sims*, were becoming vastly popular, building on the success of *Utopia, Populous, Civilization,* and *SimCity.*[80] Valve, the publisher of the seminal *Half-Life,* launched the online distribution platform Steam in 2003. This move built on the success of the modification (mod) of *Half-Life* into *Counter-Strike,* a series that today continues to be incredibly popular as an esport—played in professionalized videogame tournaments. The importance of modifications, harking back to the earlier hacking of games, continued to grow. This form of cocreation between players (or amateurs) and game workers was discovered with the launch of *World of Warcraft.* This was an immensely popular massively multiplayer online (MMO) game that required players to pay a monthly subscription and reached a peak of 10 million subscribers. Toward the end of the decade, more casual and social games like *Farmville* and *Angry Birds* became popular too, reaching millions of players via Facebook and smartphones.[81]

The 2010s saw an intensification of competition between the two main high-end consoles, now the PlayStation 4 and Xbox One, with Sony fighting it out with Microsoft. The result this time around was that the PS4 reportedly outsold the Xbox One by two to one. Despite this, the Xbox One was still a successful console (although this may be a personal view, as I bought an Xbox One early in the life cycle). This corporate struggle for dominance became harder to read as the companies stopped fully reporting on console sales, as well as breaking with the generational life cycle that had marked previous years of consoles. There were now mid-generation hardware upgrades with the PS4 Pro and Xbox One X. This had happened in the past—for example, the CD expansion for the Sega Genesis or the expansion pack for the Nintendo 64—but these updated the existing consoles, rather than introducing newer (and more expensive) versions. For Microsoft and Sony, the most profitable part of the life cycle is in the middle and later stages, so the new additions were an attempt to maximize this phenomenon. Nintendo launched the Wii U, which sold 14 million units, relatively few in comparison to the handheld 3DS, which sold 53 million units.[82] The Switch, a hybrid of mobile and home consoles, was launched later, selling 18 million in one year alone.[83]

While these console battles raged, PC gaming entered a new phase. The independently developed (indie) game *Minecraft* sold an astonishing 144 million copies (across multiple platforms, with a high of 74 million monthly players), and the developer was purchased by Microsoft for $2.5 billion.[84] The crowdfunding platform Kickstarter provided a new way for developers to raise money for games, shifting the business model of many titles. In addition to games, hardware like the virtual reality headset Oculus Rift were also funded this way. A growing number of games—including *Gone Home*, *The Last of Us*, and *Papers, Please*—began dealing with ethics and more mature themes. Today, many games offer regular downloadable content (DLC), extending or expanding the game for additional cost. Massively successful games like *Dota 2*, *League of Legends*, *CrossFire*, *Clash of Clans*, and *World of Tanks* are built on a so-called free-to-play model, in which the game itself is offered for free, but the consumer can purchase cosmetic in-game items (and sometimes things like "experience boosts") for much less than the cost of a typical game, in what are known as "microtransactions." These games make huge revenues (often far higher than those of games with an upfront cost) and have altered the business models of videogames. There has also been a rise of "gamer" brand PC hardware alongside the development of esports, as demonstrated by such ventures as Hewlett Packard's launch of the OMEN brand with its red and black aesthetic. In 2014, Amazon paid just under $1 billion to acquire Twitch, a platform upon which people livestream their own videogame play to millions.[85] Because people no longer just play videogames, but increasingly *watch others* play videogames, companies are eager to access these new audiences.

The scope, scale, technologies, revenues, audiences, and numbers relating to videogames continue to grow. When writing a history of videogames, it is hard to know when to stop. The closer we get to the present moment, the more information there seems to be about gaming, with more titles that it seems have to be mentioned. Instead of bringing the history up to right now, I want to end this section with one example that highlights the current state of videogames: *Fortnite*. The game was launched in 2017 by Epic Games and is a hybrid shooter game. While it was not the first battle royale game, it has become by far the most successful. The game is free to play, and a hundred players fight it out online, after jumping from a flying bus over an island. An estimated 135 million people have played the game; it claimed its biggest month in September 2018 (78.3 million players); and 8.3 million concurrent players were once recorded at a peak moment. The average player spends between six and ten hours per week in game, and it is estimated that players have spent $1 billion on in-game purchases.[86] While not representing all videogame play, the rise of *Fortnite* shows what an immensely popular cultural form these games have become today.

THE VIDEOGAMES
INDUSTRY

I magine you are sitting down in front of a games console. Usually you consider the sprites and animations on the screen, whether your guild members are already signed on, what mission to play next, and so on. Rarely do we consider the labor and logistics that bring us to this moment. The videogame itself involved all kinds of work to develop: coming up with the concept, story, art, missions, challenges, multiplayer dynamics, and so on. These workers crunched and worked long hours in the run-up to the long-hyped launch date—we would do well to think about who kept these workers fed, rested, and able to come back in each day ready for a long shift. There were also people who made sure the fridges were stocked and the office was clean, preparing the workplace for the next day.

Beyond the studio, workers were needed to generate media attention, advertising, and reviews. Without this, you may never have heard of the game you have chosen to play, its name lost within the huge number of games released every year. However, that decision to purchase the game also required a way to get it to you and for you to have some way to play it. The console, the cables, the screen, the controller, and so on all had to be made somewhere. It is likely they were manufactured in China, far away from where many consumers are likely to be sitting when they play. And the parts were manufactured and assembled by migrant workers who had traveled into cities from the countryside, leaving their families and communities behind. Many of these workers faced harsh and exploitative factory conditions.

You may have put a physical disk into the console or have downloaded it from a platform. Either way, the hardware needed to come together in the right way, at the right time, to end up ready in your house. The manufacture of electronics requires rare earth minerals and components from a number of countries. Imagine the web of logistics necessary to quickly and cheaply transport these to you. After the hardware traveled by road, rail, sea, or plane, you may have gone to buy the console yourself. However, you may have bought it from a company like Amazon. In that case, the decision rapidly flowed through Amazon's logistics operation, signaling the nearest worker with a GPS-enabled wristband to walk over and collect the console in one of their hubs. In under a day—or, in a major city like New York or London, in potentially under two hours—this package could have arrived at your front door. Or, the videogame could have been delivered via your internet connection, with all the hidden labor needed to maintain the physical and software infrastructure that makes this process appear so seamless.

Imagine again, you sit down at your games console to play a game. Yes, your own play may become an important part of the game if you are playing online—after all, online games are no fun if you play on your own. But imagine if all the people whose labor contributed to that moment were standing with you there too. How many people would that be? This notion, that each part of the labor process becomes "congealed" (to use Marx's term) within the videogame, gives us a sense of how complex contemporary videogame production has become.

To make sense of this, I will first examine the role of the videogames industry overall. While the work of videogame developers in studios is clearly crucial to understanding the industry, it can only properly be understood by considering it within the value chains and networks of capitalism. We can think of this development labor as a form of immaterial labor, defined as "the labor that produces the informational and cultural content of the commodity."[1] This is less material than previous forms of material work, like assembling commodities in a factory (although working on a computer still requires physical inputs and so on). This wider connection with other forms of work highlights how the videogames industry touches far more facets of contemporary life than just gaming. Nick Dyer-Witheford has captured this transformation of global class composition with the idea of the emerging "cyber-proletariat" by "taking the ideas of cybernetic thinkers as a guide to how computers in general have altered the technological processes of capital."[2] This cyber-proletariat ranges from call center operators, to miners in the Global South, to the *dagongmei* (female migrant workers) in the factories of China. I will later focus on the studio and videogame developers, but for now this discussion starts by applying a much broader lens to understand the role of the videogames industry under capitalism.

THE SCALE OF THE INDUSTRY

The scale of the contemporary videogames industry is often touted in the media. It can be difficult to ascertain the exact details, particularly as most data comes from companies who have an interest in overselling the numbers. One example is SuperData.[3] They offer reports and analysis to the industry, not, of course, for the purposes of neutral reporting, but to make a profit. If you wanted to access all of SuperData's current reports, it would cost you almost twenty thousand dollars. Unsurprisingly perhaps, I chose not to buy them. One problem with this approach is that it is not possible to independently review their findings, nor do they make their methods publicly available; the other is that the findings cost so much money to access. Nonetheless, it is useful to examine the claims they are making as it can give us a sense of the dynamics of the industry. Even if these findings do not accurately reflect the industry, they are nevertheless bought and sold, influencing decisions made by different companies. So even if not necessarily "true," they have a real effect in the world.

In 2018, the headline claim of SuperData for the previous year was that interactive entertainment generated revenues of $108.4 billion. Contained within this figure are two segments: digital gaming and interactive media. Digital gaming revenue breaks down to $59.2 billion for mobile, $33.0 billion for PC (both "premium," in which the game is purchased, and "free-to-play," meaning free to download, but players can purchase cosmetic items or "skins"), and $8.3 billion for videogame consoles. Interactive media, the smaller segment, entails $0.76 billion for esports, $3.2 billion for gaming video content, and $4.0 billion for virtual and mixed reality. The report claims that one in three people in the world (around 2.5 billion) play free-to-play games, across all platforms. Its authors argue that one of the highlights of 2017 was the launch of *PlayerUnknown's Battlegrounds*, which generated $712 million in eight months, laying the groundwork for *Fortnite*. Not only was gameplay bringing in revenue, but also people watching other people play videogames competitively, which reported 258 million unique viewers. Esports generated $756 million in revenue.[4]

These headline figures are clearly very, very large. They demonstrate that the videogames industry is both growing and mature, with huge profits to be made. The business models of many companies have also shifted within the industry, particularly with the dominance of free-to-play models. For example, free-to-play games reportedly generated $46 billion in Asia, $13.1 billion in North America, and $10.9 billion in Europe. For PC games, free-to-play took 69 percent of the $33 billion market. The top three games were Riot Games / Tencent's *League of Legends* (generating $2.1 billion), Nexon/Tencent's *Dungeon Fighter Online* ($1.6 billion), and Smilegate/Tencent's *CrossFire* ($1.4 billion). All of these are partly owned by the Chinese company Tencent, which also has a stake in five out of the top ten games. The first, *League of Legends*, is free to download, making money with optional in-game purchases.[5]

On the other hand, the "premium PC market" (games bought for an upfront price) brought in significantly less revenue. For example, in 2017 in Asia total revenue for this market was $0.3 billion; North America, $2.2 billion; and Europe, $3 billion. The top three titles included *PlayerUnknown's Battlegrounds* ($714 million—equivalent to 12 percent of all premium PC revenue), Activision Blizzard's *Overwatch* ($382 million), and Valve's *Counter-Strike: Global Offensive* ($314 million). These premium games are making much less revenue than those that can—theoretically—be played for free.

Away from the PC market, the console market remains important. It was worth $8.3 billion globally, with Asia accounting for $0.2 billion; North America, $4.2 billion; and Europe, $3.1 billion. The top three games here were Rockstar's *Grand Theft Auto V* ($521 million), Activision Blizzard's *Call of Duty: WWII* ($502 million), and EA Sports' *FIFA 17* ($409 million).[6] This pattern of consumption requires the purchasing of proprietary hardware, and, as we discussed earlier, involves competition between large companies like Sony and Microsoft.

Along with smartphones, PCs, and consoles, consumption of videogame content is now also taking place in new forms. Platforms like Twitch and YouTube are providing ways for people to watch others playing games ("streaming"), which is increasingly becoming monetized. For example, Twitch captures 54 percent of all videogaming content and revenues of $1.7 billion. YouTube accounts for 22 percent ($0.7 billion) but continues to compete. This growth in game streaming is also partly linked to the growth of esports.[7]

While these figures show the global scope of the videogames industry, it is also worth drawing attention to how these relate to national contexts. The biggest market for videogames is China, followed by the US, Japan, Germany, and the UK. The market for videogames in the US is huge, with sales of over $24.5 billion in 2016. The previous survey in 2015 showed that there were 2,457 videogame companies in the US, with 2,858 locations across every state. The industry directly employed over sixty-five thousand people, with over half of these jobs located in California, while supporting an estimated 220,000 jobs.[8]

The UK remains a smaller but nevertheless key part of the industry. According to Ukie (the trade body for the UK's games and interactive entertainment industry), it is estimated that 32.4 million people play games in the UK.[9] In 2018, a reported 2,261 active videogame companies were working in the country on projects across the industry. The UK can also claim a number of big recent successes. For example, *Grand Theft Auto V*, developed by British developer Rockstar North, is "the most financially successful media product of all time, selling over 90 million units worldwide and over $6bn in global revenue." Additionally, it "is the fastest selling entertainment product ever, grossing $1bn worldwide in just 3 days and the top selling game of all time in the UK, generating over £240m from more than 6 million physical copies sold—or roughly 3.5 sales per minute." Rockstar North, which began as DMA Design Limited, is based in Edinburgh. The UK is also home to Rocksteady Studios, developer of *Batman: Arkham Knight*, which won multiple awards and also was the fastest-selling videogame of 2015. The smartphone game *Monument Valley* was developed by Ustwo Games, a UK-based indie developer. In the two years following its release, it had been downloaded 26 million times and won twenty awards.[10]

The videogames industry, as elsewhere, has grown rapidly in the UK. From 2016 to 2017, consumer spending on games rose 12.4 percent, an estimated £5.11 billion. Of this, videogame software had a market value of £3.56 billion, with the remainder claimed by videogame hardware (£1.43 billion) and the game culture market (£117 million). Contrast this figure with the video market, £2.3 billion (of which the videogames market is 1.65 times larger); and music, £1.3 billion (videogames: 2.9 times larger).[11] Videogames therefore make up the majority (51.3 percent) of entertainment spending in the UK. This potential—and it is worth stressing that often these statistics are exaggerated—has captured the imagination of many actors, from investors to governments. For example, the British politician Boris Johnson used to write scathingly critical takes on videogames. A prominent member of the right-wing Conservative Party in the UK, he

is famous for his carefully curated image as a bumbling aristo-
crat. In an article for the right-wing British newspaper the *Tele-graph*, Johnson once wrote the following about children who play
videogames:

> They become like blinking lizards, motionless, absorbed,
> only the twitching of their hands showing they are still con-
> scious. These machines teach them nothing. They stimulate
> no ratiocination, discovery or feat of memory—though some
> of them may cunningly pretend to be educational. . . .
> So I say now: stop just lying there in your post-Christmas
> state of crapulous indifference. Get up off the sofa. Can the
> DVD of Desperate Housewives, and go to where your chil-
> dren are sitting in auto-lobotomy in front of the console.
> Summon up all your strength, all your courage. Steel your-
> self for the screams and yank out that plug. And if they still
> kick up a fuss, then get out the sledgehammer and strike a
> blow for literacy.[12]

Johnson is known for these kinds of hyperbolic takes—often quoting from classic literature and sometimes Latin. This
conservatism has been mirrored in the US (albeit without ref-
erences to either classics or Latin), with prominent politicians
railing against the violence or degeneracy of videogames. Perhaps the most interesting example of this was US state senator
Leland Yee, who was vocally anti-videogames (and particularly
anti–violent videogames) but was later jailed for involvement in
corruption and a scheme to smuggle guns into the US from the
Philippines.[13] What is interesting about these arguments is not
their substance (of course!), but the deep cynicism and paternal-
ism they entail. Johnson claimed that games were to blame for
low literacy rates, but rather than jumping on a games-cause-vi-
olence bandwagon, he advocated physical violence in response.
However, jumping forward over a decade, Johnson (now the
mayor of London) had changed his tune. In 2016, he gave a
speech to encourage the games industry in London, along with
providing it a round of funding:

We're home to fantastic software studios, like State of Play
and Sports Interactive, who make world-leading games,
like Lumino City and Football Manager. From NASA to the
NHS, games software now influences the way we manage our
health, educate our children, and even how we explore space,
but international competition remains fierce and we need to
ensure our city can compete with our global gaming rivals.
Games London will be a three-year program that will help
the game sector shout louder and attract more investment.[14]

Rather than wanting to smash up videogames, Johnson instead now sees a whole range of benefits. Similarly, in a recent
report on the games industry in the UK, George Osborne (then
the chancellor of the exchequer and also a member of the Conservative Party) decried that the games industry was "one of the
UK's great strengths" and that today is a "golden age" for the creative sector, which also included films, high-end TV, and animation programming.[15] This shift in tone, and indeed investments,
signals an important change. If we think back to the roots of the
industry, videogames have clearly come a long way. No longer
an expert's pursuit, but now something that the political representatives for the UK's ruling class see as integral to capitalism.

The games industry has undergone significant growth in recent
years, and this trend is set to continue. It is therefore unsurpris-
ing that the Conservatives quoted above are drawn to praising
and investing in the industry, particularly as the "green shoots"
of economic recovery remain hard to spot further afield. This
comes at a time when growth rates in the Global North have
been sluggish at best in the wake of the 2008 financial crisis.
In comparison with other productive sectors, it is no wonder
the videogames industry is becoming heralded as a key sector in
the economy. This has resulted in huge advantages for capital
in the form of initiatives like the Video Games Tax Relief program.[16] This has transferred £119 million to companies in over
420 claims since April 2014. Reportedly, this has been claimed
for 295 different videogames, supporting around £690 million
of expenditure in the UK.[17] In addition to these direct payments

in the UK, there has been "increasing competition by governments seeking to attract video game development studios to their jurisdictions."[18] This has resulted in a proliferation of different initiatives, from teaching coding and computer skills in schools to new funding bodies, along with accelerators, incubators, and digital catapults (although in practice, it is not clear what the difference is between the last three).

While the industry has existed in the UK since at least the 1980s, with its roots in "bedroom coding," it is now in a position of "global leadership, combining arts and technology to deliver some of the most successful games in the history of the medium."[19] For example, perhaps the most expensive videogame developed to date is *Grand Theft Auto V* (though considering the barriers of NDAs, or nondisclosure agreements, we cannot know this for certain). The development was estimated to have cost $137 million and involved 250 people working for five years. It reportedly had a budget of $265 million overall for development and marketing.[20] This is comparable with the budgets of major blockbuster films. Given these kinds of figures, it is clear why the videogames industry demands attention.

THE ROLE OF THE INDUSTRY WITHIN CAPITALISM

While the scale of the numbers above may be impressive, it is necessary to go beyond these headline figures to understand the role that the industry plays. As Aphra Kerr has explained, "Digital games cannot be understood without attention to the late capitalist economic systems from which they emerge and the changing political, social, and cultural contexts in which they are produced and consumed."[21] I now turn to discuss the role of the videogames industry within capitalism. However, it is important to remember that the videogames industry "is an exemplary global business in that its dominant organizations share a strategic orientation which exceeds any particular territorial affiliation."[22] This means that the largest videogames companies operate beyond national boundaries, combining work processes across the world to maximize profits. So *Grand Theft Auto V* can be referred to as a UK-made game and also a game *not* made in UK, with much of its production tied into value chains and networks that spread across the world. Within this vast web is "a complex competition for value capture between console manufacturers, publishers, development studios and retailers."[23] However, national differences have an effect on the production process, as "national industries where aspects of a craft ethos persist . . . make for a superior final product." This illustrates "the enduring importance of local variations in employment and working practices."[24]

Part of the problem with focusing on a national context is the lack of information available about how companies actually perform. For example, while the videogames industry is touted as a "highly innovative part of the UK's creative economy," the reality is that "hard data about its economic performance and geography are difficult to come by."[25] This, combined with the aggressive marketing and posturing of governments and trade bodies, along with the prevalence of NDAs (which we will discuss later), makes it difficult to unpack any actual details. This is further complicated by the "protean nature" of an industry in which many companies are still small, and the existence of a "pervasive start-up culture"[26]

In the UK context, only companies with over fifty employees (or over a certain turnover) have to report business data, which is why, for example, one particular trade report could only offer information on 6 percent of companies.[27] It is therefore more useful to try and understand the industry through its dynamics, rather than building up a static picture of how companies operate. The growth of the industry has to be tied to the broader shifts in the economy, particularly the decline of manufacturing and the rise of service work in the Global North. In the UK and the US, this has meant a significant increase of logistics and services, particularly in areas like retail, call centers, and deliveries. As a result, following deindustrialization and the 2008 financial crisis, most of the growth in jobs has been in low-wage and insecure employment.

The videogames industry, like other digital or creative sectors, is one that has bucked this trend. However, it remains a small part of overall employment. For example, in 2015 the core employment of the UK's videogame industry was represented by only 12,100 full-time equivalent employees. This was split between 9,400 in game development, 900 in game publishing, and 1,800 in the retail of games. These core roles contributed $1.2 billion (£755 million) directly in GVA (gross value added) to the UK economy and supported around 23,900 full-time equivalents of employment.[28] In the US there was a comparable rate of growth in 2015, but the industry brought in a far larger sum in value added to GDP—an estimated $11.7 billion (£7.7 million).[29]

The industry in the UK is composed of three different segments—development, publishing, and retail—each playing a different role. The first segment is development, without which there are no games to be published or sold. Games are made by studios, which can either be independent or owned by a publisher. The link between publisher and studio has become more complex, particularly with the emergence of alternative sources for raising capital like Kickstarter. There was, broadly speaking, around £639.1 million in GVA from development in 2013, which equates to an average of around £68,000 per worker. While this is a rough average, it does give a sense of the scope for extracting surplus value from these workers. If the average salary is lower than the amount workers are contributing, the company is clearly making a lot of money.

The second segment, publishing, is analogous to distribution in film and television. Publishing's traditional role within videogames entails funding, marketing, and distributing the finished game, involving varying levels of control between publishers and developers. The GVA from publishing in 2013 was estimated to be around £63.3 million, equating to approximately £70,000 per worker. Finally, retail involves the sale of the finished videogame. Traditionally, this entailed the sale of physical boxed games in retail space, but this is increasingly being supplanted by digital platforms. The GVA from retail was estimated to be £53 million, or around £30,000 per worker.[30] Although publishing and retail do not involve the creation of the product, they are nevertheless crucial to the realization of value from videogame production (after all, making something is not the same as making money—it still needs to be successfully sold).

This threefold understanding of the industry has been complicated by the emergence of more indie developers, many of which do not publish or retail in the same way. "Indie" lacks a clear definition but tends to involve videogames that are

> usually produced by a small group, if not a single individual, in charge of designing, developing and releasing the game. From pre- to post-production, the entire process is in the hands of one or a few persons who, in return for taking responsibility for the entire production cycle, expect to receive the complete revenues resulting from sales or in-game advertising.[31]

Despite the proliferation of indie studios, the industry remains dominated by very large companies like Sony, Microsoft, Activision Blizzard, Ubisoft, and Electronic Arts (EA). In Dyer-Witheford and de Peuter's book, they focus on EA, explaining how its "licensed-property game factories are a massive presence in the game business." In comparison to small studios, "the corporation's vertical control of production, publishing, licensing, and distribution gives it a pervasive presence." Furthermore, EA, like other large-scale corporations, "exemplifies tendencies" including those "toward concentration of ownership, repetitious licensed franchises, world-market business strategies, [and] maximizing the advantages of 'glocalization.'"[32] This can be seen clearly with the *Assassin's Creed* series, but also with FPS games and the yearly sports franchises.

In recent years, there has been a shift in which companies are making the most money from videogames. According to one report gathering estimates of top videogame revenues (excluding hardware sales), the Chinese company Tencent had revenues of $18.1 billion in 2017. It was followed by Sony, with $10.5 billion; Apple, $8 billion; Microsoft, $7.1

billion; Activision Blizzard, $6.5 billion; NetEase, $5.6 billion; Google, $5.3 billion; EA, $5.1 billion; Nintendo, $3.6 billion; and Bandai Namco, $2.4 billion. Tencent almost makes more from videogames than the second- and third-placed companies combined. Another Chinese company, NetEase, is sixth on the list. That first major shift in dominance, from the US to Japanese companies (something I discussed in my historical overview of videogames), has now been followed by a second shift that is seeing Chinese companies becoming increasingly dominant on the world level.[33] In keeping with that trend, Bungie (the American studio that developed *Destiny* for Activision) announced that it was working on a new title with NetEase, raising $100 million for development. NetEase had previously published *Minecraft* and Blizzard's games in China but is now replacing US companies in terms of funding studios.[34]

THE VIDEOGAME AS A COMMODITY

The importance of publishing in the industry must be understood in relation to the role of the videogame as commodity. Our erstwhile quest giver in *Syndicate*, Karl Marx, had this to say about commodities:

> A commodity is, in the first place, an object outside us, a thing that by its properties satisfies human wants of some sort or another. The nature of such wants, whether, for instance, they spring from the stomach or from fancy, makes no difference. Neither are we here concerned to know how the object satisfies these wants, whether directly as means of subsistence, or indirectly as means of production.[35]

Videogames do satisfy a "want" of some sort, despite the fact Marx notes it is not important what that actual "want" is. However, what is important is that videogames are a "commodity" because they are made as "a product . . . transferred to another, whom it will serve as a use value, by means of an exchange."[36] They are not (the majority of the time) made as a work of art, but rather commissioned by publishers who then seek to make returns on their investment. This can be seen most clearly with the "blockbuster" videogame series, like *Assassin's Creed*. As David Nieborg has argued, these "blockbuster" videogames, particularly on consoles, compare "well with the hit-driven nature of large parts of the movie industry. Both rely heavily on high-risk, high-return productions."[37]

The relationship between publishers and retailers determines the final price of a videogame, both for in-store and digital pricing. However, the pricing differs according to the different formats a product takes and its delivery method. The price of an Xbox One game, for example, can vary. On Amazon, through which physical games can be delivered, the price also varies substantially. At the time of this writing, recently released games cost around £49.99, which converts to around $64.[38] However, *Assassin's Creed Syndicate* (now a few years old) can be bought for £14.70/$19, whereas the newest version, *Assassin's Creed Origins*, is confusingly £36.49/$47 boxed and £54.99/$70 for a download code, even though physical box and disc are not included. The pre-orders for *Assassin's Creed Odyssey* are £49.99/$64 for the regular edition and £79.99/$102 for the "gold edition," including additional content.

Unpacking why videogames are priced the way they are can be particularly difficult, due to "the fact that so many publishers and retailers are extremely reluctant to talk about money, and especially about what happens to that money once you hand it over for a game."[39] This secretiveness was confirmed by one videogames journalist who reported not being able to get any publisher or retailer to comment on the record about pricing. Despite reducing the production and distribution costs, online downloads remain artificially pricey because publishers have to maintain relationships with retailers and "quite literally cannot afford to undercut or otherwise piss off retail under any circumstances."[40] If the publisher Ubisoft decided to undercut a physical retailer like GAME, they could refuse to stock Ubisoft's next game. Even if it did not get that far, they could threaten not to stock the game, pull back from promotion, or demand a larger cut of the sales. In each case, Ubisoft would lose money. The majority of profits are made on videogames in the weeks after they are launched, making product placement in physical locations key—along with launch events and so on.[41] As one industry analysist explained:

> For the publishers it's driven by the amount of time they have to make back their money.... On a big 100, 200-million-dollar launch, they only have 2 to 3 weeks to make back their initial investments. So it's key for publishers to have their boxes on display at the center of the store. It's all about the real estate inside the store.[42]

Similarly, this can also be found with online "real estate." For example, when searching on Amazon for "assassin's creed," the first result is "Sponsored by Ubisoft: Assassin's Creed Odyssey – Pre-order now, shop now."

This is different with PC games, as this format is rarely sold physically anymore, and the Steam distribution platform (an online storefront) is far more commonly used. The publisher-retailer relationship has therefore shifted much more cleanly to a publisher-platform relationship. Also, prices can be lower with PC games because publishers do not have to pay a license fee as they are required to do with console games (with the fee going to the console maker). Steam takes around a 30 percent cut of the sale price, whereas buying directly from a developer obviously does not involve this. It is estimated that retailers in the UK or US will take a cut of approximately 20–35 percent, although this can vary depending on what else is involved in the deal between a publisher and retailer, where, for example, discounts may be increased in exchange for in-store promotion.[43]

For the physical copy of *Assassin's Creed Origins*, analysts have offered the following breakdown of the price. If the sticker price is £49.99/$64, take away 20 percent for value-added tax and approximately 20 percent more for the retailer, leaving £29.99/$38. From this, £4.50/$5.75 is taken out for hardware royalty fees, another £4.50/$5.75 for licensed content royalties, £3/$3.80 for development costs, £1/$1.30 for manufacturing and packaging, and then optional costs of £2.40/$3.10 for price protection for returns and £1.80/$2.30 distributor costs. This leaves approximately £12.80/$16.00 in gross profit.[44] These costs vary, but it indicates that publishers can potentially make very good returns on videogames. While the retailer cut may seem high (and indeed can be much higher than indicated here), it is important to remember that "specialist shops like GAME in the UK have been really important, historically, in championing games on the high street and growing the gaming audience."[45] The same has been true in the US. Without physical retail, the videogames industry would not have grown at the same scale, which also means that development budgets would be much lower.

As discussed previously, videogame consoles are introduced in new hardware cycles, differentiating videogames from other cultural industries like film. The launch of the Xbox One and PlayStation 4 triggered the start of "a transitional phase moving from a physical, or packaged goods industry (i.e., selling boxes in retail stores) towards an on-demand circulation model based on digital distribution."[46] The large AAA games, or "triple-A" games (those with the highest development and marketing budgets), pushed by publishers were no longer single purchase, but rather became "a hybrid product, signaling the mixture of physical and digital circulation mechanisms."[47] This generation of consoles facilitated the distribution of DLC (downloadable content), which is one way that publishers have tried to get around their relationship with retailers to extract more profit from videogames. "DLCs" are additions to games that are sold after the purchase of the boxed game. Often, they involve additional missions or maps, increasing the longevity of the game.

In 2015, it was also clear from EA's financial reports why it was so keen on DLCs. EA made twice as much money from DLCs as it did with full games that were downloaded. In 2015, the *FIFA* soccer game was mainly bought in store (around 80 percent of copies). EA made less on these physical copies for the reasons outlined above. However, DLCs brought in even more than the online copies (which have already removed the physical retailer cut). In one quarter in 2015, EA made $89 million from digital game sales (it did not release figures for physical sales, although it is estimated to be around $450 million) but made $195 million from "extra content."[48] Following up on the potential to make money in this way, EA has launched its own proprietary online store, "Origin"; Ubisoft has launched a store; and Activision Blizzard has the Battle.net launcher.

One way to understand the DLC phenomenon is to focus on the way in which AAA games have become commodified. As David Nieborg has argued, these kinds of videogames can be theorized as cultural commodities. This involves unpacking how the "cultural product's use value is transformed into exchange value," focusing on "what kind of Triple-A games are made, under what conditions, and how they are circulated."[49] What Nieborg argues, which is particularly convincing, is that AAA games are "best understood as an incremental and seemingly infinite stream of renewable gaming experiences. Furthermore, the AAA game in its commodity form functions fully inside a capitalist framework, and it is hence tied into a specific production and circulation logic." In terms of console games, this means understanding the determining effects of the "console game's platform-dependent nature," including the limitations of the hardware, software, game controllers, and graphical user interfaces. These standardize the game production process, closing down possibilities of the kinds of games that are commissioned and made. As Ian Bogost has explained, "These confines both facilitate and limit discursive production, just as the rules of natural languages bound poetry and the rules of optics bound photography."[50]

The result is "two clearly discernible, complementary formatting strategies" for AAA games. The first is franchising, with regular serialization tied into publishing frameworks to maximize revenue. The second is the use of "digitally distributed content," which leverages the capacity of these consoles to generate further revenue. Both economics and the technology of proprietary systems (itself a function of the economics of the hardware owners) have an important effect on videogame production. These shape the kinds of games that emerge, ensuring that high levels of capital investment combine with these new distribution methods to make money out of games as cultural products.[51] However, as videogames move beyond the console, the digital distribution part of this business model has become increasingly dominant.

The publisher Valve first developed Steam in 2003 as a way to keep its game *Counter-Strike* updated and to ensure that individual users had the same playable version of the game. With the launch of *Half-Life 2* the year after, Steam became a way for Valve to sell directly to consumers. Valve then later opened the platform up to third-party sellers—now the platform is estimated to control as much as 70 percent of digital PC videogame sales.[52] It can be difficult to get accurate figures for Steam, but the third-party website Steam Spy scrapes data from Steam to create estimates. In 2017, there were 7,672 videogames released on Steam, a big increase from the 4,207 released in 2016 (which accounted for 38 percent of all videogames the online distributor had released to date); it was preceded by increases from 2,964 in 2015, 1,772 in 2014, and only 565 in 2013.[53] For the consumer, Steam offers a way to find videogames in one place (or at least try to find them, given the huge number of products). For Valve, the platform offers a way to form a near-monopoly over PC online videogame distribution.

Of course, monopolistic tendencies within media—or other industries for that matter—have been pursued previously, but, as Daniel Joseph has argued, Steam represents a new attempt at this old practice.[54] Steam acts as a platform. As Nick Srnicek argues, platforms "position themselves as intermediaries that bring together different users . . . and more often than not, these platforms also come with a series of tools that enable their users to build their own products, services, and marketplaces."[55] The overwhelming majority of the games being sold on Steam were produced by other companies. Platforms do not just host content; they seek to make money (in the form of rent—a payment for the temporary use of a good, service, or property).

To most users, Steam appears to be a slick and well-designed interface. As Joseph points out, "Code works when it slides by in the background, working its numbers while nobody talks about it." However, when conflicts appear, it is also possible to "see this social relation for what it is: control."[56] The practices of modding are one example of this. Modding is generally accepted by videogame companies, so long as the modder does not then sell the game that was modified. This brings a user, who was initially only a player, onto the platform as a kind of unpaid worker. Steam hosts mods as part of its distribution service, with users free to download and experiment with other users' creations.

However, in 2015, Valve and Bethesda decided to implement a way to sell mods through the Steam platform. The code was changed, altering how mods were distributed, introducing paid mods. This had knock-on effects for mods that relied on other mods—if the latter were no longer free, that called into question whether the former could remain free too. Ultimately, this meant the commodification of what had previously been a hobby relationship for many. As Joseph put it, the "mod community then collectively lost its shit."[57] Alongside widespread protests, the modders "stopped working, and the power enabled by that code fell apart. This wasn't [necessarily] understood consciously as class struggle, but it could have been under different circumstances."[58] The modders' action convinced Valve and Bethesda to reverse the decision. However, Valve announced in 2018 that it would be partnering with Perfect World Games to bring the Steam platform to China, continuing the push toward monopoly.[59] The driving force, as Joseph points out, "remains the same as Karl Marx laid out in *Capital*: the exploitation of labor to produce surplus value." As disconcerting as this drive is, this is not the only kind of conflict over videogames.

THE MILITARY-INDUSTRIAL COMPLEX

The conflict over videogames is not only between workers and capital at different points of the production and distribution process, nor is it limited to wars between rival console makers or different publishers. Videogames have long had a connection with war itself through the military. This is a continuation of the way "games and war have always stood in a close relationship to one another," from board games like chess and Go to strategy videogame, gladiatorial competitions, and FPS games.[60] A body of research on the military-entertainment complex has unveiled organizational links between armies and games and explored the effects on players.[61] Less attention has been paid to how military games are actually produced, and to understanding how the individual labor processes combine to create the final product.

The military saw the early potential for videogames to train soldiers and try out strategies, as with earlier kinds of war games that have been used extensively in the history of war. For example, in the 1980s, the Defense Advanced Research Projects Agency (DARPA) began working with developers to make training games. Similarly, as a way to train the US Marine Corps, they modified *Doom II*, renaming it *Marine Doom*. The military later continued with this idea through extensive iterations, including *Virtual Battlespace 2*, used to train "thousands of troops sent to Afghanistan."[62] Similarly, the British military has "had to radically improve some of its simulated training war games to keep the attention of recruits" who grew up with the latest videogames.[63] The connection therefore strengthens through "game developers and war planners" having "overlapping interests in multimedia simulation and virtual experience," resulting in greater collaboration and the subsidization of the production of new games.[64] This has involved direct crossovers between the games industry and the military—for example, a recruitment ad for the British Army features an unbranded Xbox controller flying a drone.[65]

The military's modification of games went further with the launch of the *America's Army* series and *Full Spectrum Warrior*. *America's Army* was published by the US Army and designed as a recruitment tool adapted and suited to the next generation of videogame-playing youth. This direct connection was continued with *Full Spectrum Warrior*, which was used as a training tool.[66]

The subsumption of videogames has therefore involved forming an industry to create and sell games to serve particular purposes and interests. FPS games are therefore one part of the "manifestation of a larger thematic complex that focuses gaming culture on the subject-positions and discourses of what" can be termed "militarized masculinity."[67] These kinds of videogames are made by people with links (direct or indirect) to the military, and sometimes even used directly to train or recruit people.

The growth of the military videogames industry has been captured by Roger Stahl as a form of "militainment" that involves "state violence" being "translated into an object of pleasurable consumption. Beyond this, it also suggests that this state violence is not of the abstract, distant, or historical variety but rather an impending or current use of force, one directly relevant to the citizen's current political life."[68] Militainment is something that has a long history and is commonly found in film and other mediums. Clearly, it benefits the army and the state in normalizing military action, but in this case, the approach to game development is sometimes less clear-cut than the US Army simply publishing its own game. More often, games developers rely on the expertise of military consultants and thus do not have "to submit their design choices to the scrutiny of the government's exacting review processes."[69]

The process of finding military consultants proved easy for the developers of *Call of Duty*. As one of the developers explained: "We've been fortunate that the series has a lot of fans across military organizations, and within the entertainment industry." They continued to note that "this draws a lot of interest, and a great deal of desire to help *Call of Duty*."[70] The use of consultants has a long history in the film industry, but Keith Stuart rightly poses the question of whether developers should "be mining real-world expertise for narrative authenticity."[71] Thus far, this question has been overshadowed by the drive for realism, with the formalization of the process through the establishment of companies like Strike Fighter Consulting, which offers expertise ranging "from fighter pilots, bomber pilots, and test pilots to mission commanders, intelligence specialists and special operation forces."[72] As its marketing materials explain, "military consultants" can help developers "create lifelike combat scenarios that"—they claim—"will ultimately lead to more immersive gameplay and higher sales."[73] However, offering an "unfiltered view from 'the trenches'" has also proved problematic in practice. The use of US Navy SEALs in *Medal of Honor: Warfighter* apparently involved divulging classified information, leading to official letters of reprimand.[74] This "unfiltered view" appeared to involve information to which the public was not even supposed to be have access.

Consultants are not the only way that connections are made between game developers and the military-industrial complex. Although most consumers are probably unaware of this, many developers pay gun manufacturers to include their products in games. As I noted in the earlier discussion of the costs for making a videogame earlier, one component is the payment of royalties, which in some cases gun manufacturers will partly cover. The popularity of videogames as a medium has also meant they are increasingly attracting the attention of advertisers. In esports competitions, for example, companies selling computer parts and peripherals will regularly act as sponsors and advertisers, and now non-endemic companies are becoming involved too. Simon Parkin notes the history of companies sponsoring "imitation adult products to children," citing the examples of candy cigarettes and Gibson's licensing of plastic guitars. While this approach may make sense with computer peripherals in general, or sports cars in racing games, or even equipment in sports games, this is not as obvious in videogames about war—particularly when many gamers are children. However, perhaps this may not come as so much of a surprise to readers in the US as it does to someone living in Britain, a country in which the idea of buying a gun is almost as unlikely as seeing an advert for one. Parkin found that "licensed weapons are commonplace in video games, but the deals between game makers and gun-manufacturer are shrouded." None of the publishers he contacted were prepared to discuss the practice.[75]

Despite publishers' unwillingness to discuss this issue, information can be gathered from the other side of the deal. Cybergun, a French company, has built on its experience of making BB guns (which often look like real weapons) to negotiate deals between gun manufacturers and game developers, including acting for "Uzi, Kalashnikov, Colt, FAMAS, FN Herstal, Sig Sauer, Mauser and Taurus." However, Barrett—the creators of the M82 sniper rifle—were much more forthcoming with details, with a representative explaining that "video games expose our brand to a young audience who are considered possible future owners."[76] It was also revealed that the negotiable royalty fee could either be a one-off payment or a percentage, perhaps as high as 5 to 10 percent of the game's retail price.[77]

Despite the commodification of increasingly greater numbers of things under capitalism, it is still surprising to hear that a .50-caliber rifle is being marketed to children. From the viewpoint of someone living in Britain, it is hard to think of a plausible reason for a person to purchase a rifle so large and powerful it is designed to disable vehicles with a single shot to the engine block. But regardless, it *should* still be hard to justify marketing it to children.

The negotiation on a gun's inclusion in a game can also go beyond the financial details. In the case of Barrett, this means the company can rest assured it knows "explicitly how the rifle is to be used, ensuring that we are shown in a positive light . . . such as the 'good guys' using the rifle."[78] No developer would be able to feature the gun being used by actors designated as enemies of the US or on proscribed terrorist lists. This could result in the rewriting of history to fit the requirements. For example, the South Armagh Brigade of the IRA successfully used the Barrett rifle against both the British Army and the Royal Ulster Constabulary in the 1990s. In a game featuring this particular brigade, the gun would have to be removed.

Many arms companies have sold their products across a variety of conflicts, with the UK exporting over £7 billion of arms annually, and often to "repressive regimes."[79] However, the issue of who are considered "friends" and "enemies" serves the interests of the state, and is now reinforced in videogames too. As a result, "consumers have, for the past few years, unwittingly funded arms companies that often have their own military agendas."[80] This raises serious ethical concerns, blurring the distinction between game and reality. For example, Martin Hollis, previously a developer of violent videogames, explained that since his change of heart, his "moral position" is that "you are partially complicit with violence as soon as you have a violent narrative.... Licensing gun names is a darker point on a spectrum that begins with the act of playing Cops and Robbers. But putting money in the palm of arms dealers can only help them make tools to kill."[81] Yet, this discussion is never present in the hyperbolic debates on videogame violence held by politicians and other public figures.

The success of contemporary videogames like *Call of Duty* has also led to this relationship between the industry and the military becoming even more reciprocal. Dave Anthony, a writer and producer on the *Call of Duty* games, was invited to participate in the Atlantic Council—a US think tank that "advises on the future of unknown conflict." By participating in the making of a videogame about the future of war, Anthony then began to participate in the actual planning of future conflict. His first suggestion was closer to home: the "introduction of school marshals, 'U.S. soldiers who are in plainclothes, whose job is to protect schools.'"[82]

These connections between the military-industrial complex and the videogames industry go beyond simply consulting. In some cases, the coordination involves the direct involvement of the military, whereas in others it entails indirect involvement, including payment. However, this development marks an important divergence between the development of AAA games and that of indie games, particularly with regard to the differential levels of resources and (potential) access of AAA developers to military sources of funding.

In light of all of these considerations, it is increasingly important to understand how these kinds of games are *actually* being made. What is needed is a materialist analysis to explore how the military and capital, in various ways, enter into or affect the process of producing games and the content they include. It is to the studio environment, where most videogames are made, that I will turn to next.

THE WORK OF VIDEOGAMES

On *Game Dev Story*, the player takes control of a videogame development company. Originally released for Windows over twenty years ago, it was more recently ported to smartphones. It uses a typical setup from the management genre: you watch over a workplace, taking unilateral decisions and allocating resources. However, rather than running a corporation or building a city, this game has you developing videogames. With its pixel art direction, the game offers a certain indie vibe as you set off on making your own digital creations.

The game-making process begins by selecting "develop" and "new game." Quite straightforward so far. This allows the player to select the "platform"—for example, "PC game." The "genre"—for example, "adventure"—is then combined with a "type," such as "pirate." Each example has a popularity rating from A to C, and these need to be combined to make a game that will sell. This allows for some odd combinations, though unfortunately, the game has not provided options for "management" and "video game studio," thus avoiding the potential scenario of spiraling into a meta-loop of imagining whether you as a player (managing a studio) should make a game about managing a studio, and whether there are enough imagined potential customers who would want to play a game about managing a studio.

There are then some choices to make for "direction," either "normal" or "quality," which comes with additional costs, and so on. From here, the player can add points to the direction, choosing to increase such qualities as "cuteness," "realism," "approachability," "niche appeal," "simplicity," "innovation," "game world," and "polish." After making these selections, the player begins in dialogue with the secretary, who says, "Congratulations on starting your first game!"

The actual making of the game then requires someone to write the proposal, either using "a scenario writer on staff" or hiring "an outside expert." If selecting staff, they then reply, "A pirate game? I'll try and make something that's never been done before!" As they sit at their desk typing away, small icons pop up over their head: a gamepad signifying "fun," a gold ball for "creativity," a palette for "graphics," and a trumpet for "sound." Their activity adds to the game's ongoing numerical total, which is displayed at the bottom of the screen. The player's view returns the perspective to the whole studio, with each of the workers taking a desk. As they sit and work, more icons begin to appear, as well as a purple monster head for "bugs" (software defects). There is no way to actively manage the workers in the studio, though a percentage indicator tracks their progress. Occasionally a worker may catch on fire—not literally, but as an indication that they are working particularly well—adding more points to the game. Once the progress tracker reaches 100 percent, the game can be released. A magazine pop-up displays four game reviewers (each with their own pixel art portrait). They say things like "Hmm" as the numbers randomly change. Each gives a one-line comment—"Title screen wasn't bad" or "Rethink the combination"—and a score on a scale of one to ten.

Once the imagined game is designed, produced, and reviewed, *Game Dev Story* moves on to a sales simulation, during which the player is presented with various aspects of marketing their new product. This includes taking out ads, training more staff, and so on, all while managing the studio. The process includes outsourcing, something that is increasingly common in the industry. However, while it covers lots of activities, it also—perhaps unsurprisingly—simplifies and misses out on much of the real process of making a videogame.

One key difference is that the development process in the game is sequential, with each activity neatly compartmentalized. The real process is much more complicated and messy. The action in *Game Dev Story* "ultimately boils down to two simple acts: selecting various menu items, and watching various meters fill up."[1] Decisions are easily made, and the development process is linear. Workers have clearly defined skills and can be motivated in a straightforward way. The game is set up "so your character, resting at a desk on the top left of the screen, does absolutely nothing. He just sits back and watches as his staff does all the work."[2] One way to read this feature of the game's design is that in a simulation in which the player controls from above, the workers do not need to be motivated or cajoled into action. The other could be that management, as in real life, does not in fact add to the game-making process other than picking a genre and type.

Game Dev Story is a simulation, not intended to provide an entirely accurate representation of how a videogame is *actually* made. However, it is useful to think about the image of game development presented here and the glimpse it provides into a virtual workplace. Clearly, the development studio is not a factory, neither a contemporary one nor one of Victorian Britain. However, following on from Marx's encounter with the Frye twins in *Assassin's Creed Syndicate* (as well as what he actually tried in real-life London), we can think about what inquiring into the conditions in the videogame studio might mean. So far, we have drawn on the reports about the industry, but this has only sketched out the history of the industry and its roles within capitalism. What I turn to now is a Marxist focus on the labor process—how videogames are made—to understand the *work of play*.

THE CHALLENGE OF INQUIRING INTO VIDEOGAME WORK

One of the major challenges here is that the work of making videogames is often hidden. The experience that many of us have playing videogames is quite different to the experience of making a game itself. The top-down perspective in the studio of *Game Dev Story* does not have an equivalent in the real-life studio. The act of writing code has become mystified to many of us, and so the coordination among thousands of software developers, designers, artists, scriptwriters, voice actors, audio technicians, and so on becomes even more complex. This occurs before the game development work in the studio is linked to the networks of publishing, marketing, sales, productions, and logistics upon which the industry relies.

It is no accident that the details of making videogames can be hard to come by. In the games industry—like the tech industry more broadly—there is a prevalence of NDAs (nondisclosure agreements). These have become a common and mostly accepted part of employment contracts in the industry, mainly because "big business likes to talk on its own terms, in video games as elsewhere," though "to someone standing outside the games industry looking in, this might seem strange and intimidating."[3] Initially, these contract clauses were used as a way for management to control the flow of information about a project—a particularly important priority for major forthcoming videogames, which are competing with other titles and have huge marketing budgets. However, once NDAs became widespread, they had a knock-on effect of preventing workers from talking about anything related to their work. While Marx never had to deal with NDAs for factory workers, he would have clearly disapproved of the law being used to silence workers.

To illustrate how important controlling information is for videogame companies, we can draw again on *Assassin's Creed Syndicate*. When Kotaku (a website that often covers videogame news) reported on the as-of-then unannounced videogame, it was effectively blacklisted by the publisher Ubisoft. This move—along with Kotaku's blacklisting by Bethesda, another large publisher—meant the website was denied access to upcoming games (often sent out for review before launch) and the company's official PR effort. As the editor in chief of Kotaku explained at the time:

We told the truth about [the publishers'] games, sometimes in ways that disrupted a marketing plan, other times in ways that shone an unflattering light on their products and company practices. Both publishers' actions demonstrate contempt for us and, by extension, the whole of the gaming press. They would hamper independent reporting in pursuit of a status quo in which video game journalists are little more than malleable, servile arms of a corporate sales apparatus.[4]

If this is the extent to which publishers are prepared to go to prevent information about forthcoming games, it is not hard to imagine how this approach could also be used to suppress information about how games are being made. This use of NDAs acts as an initial block to research, the sharing of information for purposes of comparison, and, of course, organizing. As an anonymous game developer explained, "I've lost count of the number of cold calls I've had from recruiters who can't actually say what a project is, only that 'I'll like it.'" They continued: "In interviews a couple of times, I've signed an NDA before I even took off my coat in a studio, and by the time I leave I still have no idea what they actually wanted to hire me for." It is hard to imagine going to an interview without being told (or then being able to share) the details of a job in many other industries. This level of security is usually reserved for working for a spy agency. The burden of the NDA on the employee remains once the actual work has begun, as the developer explained: "When something really shit is going down, it's stressful to not have the option to turn to other devs outside of the studio you're working for, for advice . . . not just about the game, but about internal politics."[5]

Often NDAs can be justified to protect particular aspects of a job, perhaps sensitive customer or business data, but in many cases they are applied to other aspects of work. The use of NDAs therefore creates serious problems for workers themselves, because in addition to making it difficult for outsiders to understand the work of the industry, it isolates workers from each other. It makes the act of complaining around the watercooler, an integral part of so many jobs (whether the meeting point is an actual

watercooler or not), significantly harder. This means that workers can have a harder time dealing with issues of stress. There
are stories of developers "working themselves into the ground and
feeling unable to discuss the problem for fear of social isolation
from colleagues or even litigation from their employer."[6] This
roadblock to sharing information acts as an obstacle to organizing, an attempt to prevent early moments of resistance from
growing. It also makes it difficult to conduct official collaborative
research on the conditions of work in the videogames industry,
because the first step in gaining access to companies is always to
sign an extensive NDA—preventing the publication of findings
without the company reviewing them, for example.

It is also important to note that NDAs, if complied with, create
a serious hindrance for videogame workers, but if *not* complied
with, can be a great source of potential strength. We should remember that information leaked by developers can now "reach
millions of people within minutes."[7] The release of such sensitive
information—or even the threat of doing so—represents a very
powerful weapon that videogame workers possess.

Before understanding how, or indeed why, different kinds
of struggles could emerge within the videogames industry, we
need to think about what an inquiry would mean in this context.
Clearly, the use of NDAs needs to be challenged in the workplace
because they obstruct employees' access to information and vital forms of communicating with each other—but this is always
an issue with work in general, to a greater or lesser extent. For
example, when Marx metaphorically followed the worker and
capitalist into what he called the "hidden abode of production,"
he notes that a sign on the threshold declares, "No admittance
except on business."[8] We are going to ignore that sign, like Marx
did, to metaphorically walk into the studio and find out how
games are made, along with who makes them.

THE NEW FACTORY INSPECTORS

Before we get to discussing the work in studios, I want to return to our encounter with Marx in *Assassin's Creed*. Marxism has so far helped to sketch out the overall shape of the industry, but it also offers another way we can look critically at work. Although this might sound like a diversion from the subject of videogames, it will provide the foundation for how we can make sense of the work as well as how workers are beginning to organize.

In Marx's time, he drew on the reports of factory inspectors to examine workers' conditions. Unlike in *Syndicate*, Marx did not need an assassin or some other operative to steal the reports. Instead, they were published and publicly available. The reports' data allowed Marx to write the fantastic tenth chapter of *Capital*, in which he detailed how the length of the working day is decided through the struggle between workers and capitalists.[9] This chapter reads like Engels's *Condition of the Working Class in England*—a damning indictment of work under capitalism.[10] As David Harvey has argued, Marx "would not have been able to write this chapter without the abundant information" supplied by the factory inspectors.[11] This is evident in Marx's own comments about the "'ruthless' factory inspector Leonard Horner" whose "services to the English working class will never be forgotten."[12]

It may sound a little odd that Marx would rely on these bourgeois factory inspectors, or even that such inspectors would exist at the time. For different reasons, both Marx and the inspectors wanted to understand the working day. For the inspectors, this was about approaching workers the same way one would handle other factors of production, such as, for example, ensuring soil is not depleted for agriculture. The inspectors were civil servants, acting on the orders of the capitalist state—not searching for material to aid in its overthrow. Marx, on the other hand, had quite different intentions for drawing on the factory inspectors' reports. He did not write *Capital* just to document bad working conditions. As Harry Cleaver has argued, it is important to remember "Marx's original purpose: he wrote *Capital* to put a weapon in the hands of workers."[13] It was a book written for the workers' movement, but it focused on capital—rather than workers—precisely because, "given the inherent mystification of capital, demystification is a necessary condition for workers to go beyond capital."[14] We can therefore start with *Capital* to understand videogames, too, as an attempt to demystify the industry. However, as Michael Lebowitz argues, there is also a "silence" for most of *Capital* when it comes to the experience of workers, as it attempts to explain "the logic of capital but not the logic of wage-labour."[15] Only chapter 10 of the book offers a very cutting, though brief, focus on workers' experience.

Later in his life, Marx experimented with a way to go beyond the silence of *Capital* noted by Lebowitz. Rather than speaking himself to this silence, Marx published a call for a workers' inquiry in a French newspaper in 1880, trying to solicit responses from workers. In the introduction to the survey, Marx explains:

> We hope to meet in this work with the support of all workers in town and country who understand that they alone can describe with full knowledge the misfortunes from which they suffer, and that only they, and not saviors sent by Providence, can energetically apply the healing remedies for the social ills to which they are a prey.
>
> We also rely upon socialists of all schools who, being wishful for social reform, must wish for an exact and positive knowledge of the conditions in which the working class— the class to whom the future belongs—works and moves.[16]

In this introduction, Marx moves from the position of *Capital* to something quite different. Workers are not considered as people just to be inspected—instead they are understood as people with agency and the power to change their own circumstances. Marx wanted to do more than just produce data; he wanted to make contact with workers. For example, he emphasized that "the name and address should be given so that if necessary we can send communication."[17]

Workers' inquiry is therefore an examination of workers' "actual struggles: their content, how they have developed, and where they are headed."[18] This correction was meant to fill the silence of *Capital* with the noise of class struggle, a sound we will be listening to closely for the remainder of this book. Marx's ideas about workers' inquiry were taken up again by later socialists.[19] These different attempts—taking in mass production, car factories, chemical works, and even insurance companies—were able to shed light on changes in work and how workers were resisting and organizing. The strongest examples come from the Italian tradition of Workerism, which has been drawn upon to develop a method of understanding contemporary workplaces, like my own attempt at an inquiry in a call center.[20]

Workers' inquiry has become a way to access, understand, and organize with workers. An important distinction to make here is between what is called inquiry "from above" and inquiry "from below." Conducting a study from outside would be considered "from above"—for example, using questionnaires or setting up interviews. However, the potential of workers' inquiry as a method goes way beyond this. The "from below" approach means drawing workers into a process of "co-research," breaking down the barrier between researcher and researched, deeply connecting the process of knowledge construction with workers' organization.[21]

In addition to these approaches to how to conduct an inquiry, Italian Workerism also provides a way to make sense of the results of an inquiry. This is the idea of "class composition." The editors of the publication *Notes from Below*—of which I am one—have updated this framework to expand on the concept of class composition, which they view as

> a material relation with three parts: the first is the organisation of labour-power into a working class (technical composition); the second is the organisation of the working class into a class society (social composition); the third is the self-organisation of the working class into a force for class struggle (political composition).[22]

This framework expands the understanding of class composition to include workers beyond the workplace. I will now take up this threefold understanding to understand the class composition of videogame workers. The sections that follow are the start of an inquiry into the industry, taking in the "new" inspectors of the industry, along with an ongoing organizing project of videogame workers.

TECHNICAL COMPOSITION

Starting from outside the workplace, we can sketch out the overall dynamics of the videogames industry. This means exploring the technical composition and trying to understand the labor process and work conditions in videogame studios. In my earlier discussion of the history of videogames, one of the features I highlighted was the role of hackers, amateurs, and the use of technology *against* its original intention. This modding of videogames (changing or adding to them) remains an important component of how videogames are made today. People whose relationship to the videogames industry is closer to that of a player than a formal worker still contribute their labor in various ways. Some of the biggest videogames—*Counter-Strike, League of Legends, Dota 2*—began as mods for existing games before they were professionalized and extended. This form of labor has been conceptualized as "playbour."[23] It is a combination of play and labor that signals how the activity of modders is contradictory: "simultaneously voluntarily given and unwaged, enjoyed and exploited."[24]

The roots of modding remain important to the contemporary videogame industry. For example, Valve began with *Half-Life*, which was built on a heavily modified version of the *Quake 2* game engine. This was later modded by Minh "Gooseman" Le, then a university student, in collaboration with fellow students. The game they created in 1999, *Counter-Strike*, was later purchased by Valve, with Le working for the company. In the process *Counter-Strike* was absorbed by the company, becoming a series that has had huge global success. However, this shift from amateur to professional does not come without issues. The problem with the process is that "the modders' leisure is being commodified by the games industry," meaning the original formulation of playbour was "precarious playbour."[25] Within the scope of the contemporary industry, this experimentation that was present at the birth of videogames is increasingly being consumed under the demands of the industry. Playbour, therefore, "continues the tradition of hacker culture from which games sprang, transforming it from esoteric art into a more general capacity for autoproduction, networked collaboration, and self-organization."[26]

Alongside this unpaid work that contributes to videogames is a range of paid work that is often hidden too. As production scales up over a global level, the outsourcing of work has become particularly prevalent. This is "a less-visible facet of the globalization of game production," which includes "tasks that are farmed out," including "'porting' existing games to additional platforms, rote programming, and made-to-order artwork."[27] This involves new divisions of labor, shifting less profitable or more routine aspects of development to different parts of the world. This kind of hidden immaterial labor is performed by "below the line game workers." In the Global North, the line separates these workers from the more "glamorous" aspects of videogame developers, which rely on the work of those "below the line."[28] This involves work like testing games, which, although in theory it sounds like the kind of job many would have wanted as a child, it is a much less glamorous and repetitive kind of work, necessary for ensuring that the finished videogame is ready. Often the workers "are hoping to join the above the line club," putting up with precarious conditions and low pay with the promise of later promotion.[29] As one worker explained:

> I was a quality assurance tester at Rockstar, and at its worst, we worked 72 hours a week. I was one of the unlucky ones to be working the night shifts. That's 8pm–8am, six days a week, testing *Grand Theft Auto*. It was horrendous. I didn't see daylight for months. This was perceived as a requirement and if you had issues with it, you were told "Well, you can

go stack shelves at Tesco instead or answer phones at a call centre." You were treated as disposable.[30]

Many of these forms of work "below the line" are gendered in various ways. For example, in the increasingly important area of publicity and marketing, in which publishers compete in ever more crowded marketplaces for videogames, the sector is "solidly pink-collar," with public relations workers over 85 percent female. However, in contrast to how journalists are respected for their creative work, publicists have often become targeted as "spin doctors" that are "an insidious and growing threat to journalism and democracy."[31] The nature of the work involves organizing press releases, managing social media, planning events, and so on, all of which relies on relationship building. The labor process in public relations therefore entails "certain overlap of professional and personal relationships" that "is not only likely, but ideal."[32] Unlike the passion often found with workers in the videogames industry, at its core public relations involves the "expression of enthusiasm for a product because of pay rather than passion."[33] It is a kind of emotional or affective labor, in which the publicist seeks to generate attention for a product. This has led to criticisms by journalists of the "phoniness" of publicity—that the workers themselves might not actually *feel* as strongly about the product or videogame as they profess. In an industry that puts so much emphasis on passion, the "unspoken heart of [the journalists'] criticism is the failure on the part of the publicist to adequately conceal that she is performing emotional work for money."[34] Yet without this form of work, videogames could go unnoticed, despite the quality of work put in through the development stage.

Another aspect of this kind of relational or emotional labor is found in the work required to maintain videogame communities, with more women likely to be working in these roles than in the field of development.[35] This work includes in-game support, online forums, message boards, meet-ups, conventions, and so on. For example, community management has grown significantly as companies recognize the importance of communities for the long-term sustainability of videogames. The work "relies heavily on native language, cultural knowledge, soft skills, experience, and gaming knowledge."[36] Workers are expected to manage the community, understanding its members' needs and demands as well as managing expectations. With an online game, this might involve ensuring players are happy with the gameplay, and that they are kept informed about scheduled updates that change aspects of the game. This can mean mediating disputes, criticisms, and crises, along with ensuring that members of the community feel heard. This is particularly important for the online videogames around which active communities are formed. Community managers have to use their skills to "mediate a range of problematic user behaviors," ensuring that a healthy community is developed and sustained. This involves "passion, community, and online social relationships" that are "employed directly in both the recruitment and the logics of cultural production," and therefore crucial to many videogames.[37] Yet, despite this important role, "their creativity, translation, reporting, and management skills are undervalued while flexibility and instability are common."[38]

If there is a line between the different kinds of immaterial labor, it is very important to remember that there is another line that separates forms of immaterial and material labor. This line is longer and obscures even more than the immaterial labor line, as all of the types of work below it rely on an "all-too-material labor far from the game studio, in electronics factories, e-waste dumps, and coltan mines."[39] Videogames, whether for computers or consoles, require hardware both to be made and to be played, which relies upon physical production and logistic networks. This involves labor that is "industrial and bluntly material: extruding plastics and sheet metal for box enclosure, connecting cables, installing circuit boards, attaching shells, and checking production flow."[40] The conditions under which hardware is made are deeply exploitative; with the *dagongmei* of China, as detailed by Pun Ngai,[41] this situation is much closer to that of the industrial workers in Marx's *Capital* than of the employees at a videogame studio or tech campus workplace.[42]

While the videogame studio is a very different environment, it is still a site of exploitation. Although challenges of NDAs make studios hard to access, overall details can be gathered from developer surveys, whose data may suggest stable work conditions, but a general precarity often hides within the figures.

A 2017 survey published by the International Game Developers Association (IGDA) helped identify key characteristics of the videogames industry. (The survey had an international focus but heavily featured responses from the US.) For example, it showed that 30 percent of employees worked at companies of between 101 to 500 people and 18 percent at companies of 500 or more. The rest worked at medium-sized studios with 11 to 50 (22 percent) and smaller studios with 10 or fewer (18 percent). The numbers show there is not one typical workplace size. Within the broad span of large companies and smaller indie studios, the size of the development teams differs too: survey data revealed that 24 percent had development teams of more than 50 people, 31 percent had between 11 and 50, and 45 percent 10 or fewer.[43]

In terms of compensation, industry workers report comparatively high average incomes. The majority of workers (54 percent) made over fifty thousand dollars a year, with 15 percent making between seventy-five thousand dollars and one hundred thousand dollars a year. In addition, there was a prevalence of bonuses and other forms of remuneration. Lump sum payments were received by 40 percent of workers, company equity by 24 percent, and royalties for the success of games by 20 percent.

The sample indicated that the majority of workers were on permanent contracts (70 percent), with only 3 percent on temporary contracts. Apart from this group, 19 percent were self-employed, and 8 percent worked as independent contractors or freelancers. The overwhelming majority (89 percent) worked full time in the industry. However, these figures can paint a deceptively rosy picture. While the 70 percent of workers on permanent contracts may sound like stable employment, respondents had an average of

2.2 employers over the past five years, while independent contractors and freelancers were hired by 3.6, and the self-employed had contracts with 2.9.[44] It is therefore possible to deduce that those in the category with which one would expect stability (permanent contracts) are likely to experience surprisingly high turnover, while those in the categories that one would expect the most flexibility (independent contractor, freelancer, and self-employed) have surprisingly stable relationships. This implies that there may well be issues "about the misclassification and misuse of freelance/independent contract labour," as companies "may be skirting the definitions of freelance or independent contractor to hire de facto employees while avoiding regulatory regimes and payroll costs."[45]

Within these studios, the workers making videogames are not sitting at desks while icons pop over their heads, as in *Game Dev Story*. But they do, in large part, look quite like the stereotypical image of the videogame worker: "youthful, predominantly male, technically wizard, sceptical towards suits, outside the union traditions, and ideologically in varying proportions, libertarian, entrepreneurial and idealist."[46] The kind of work being undertaken today draws, as it has historically, on the "hard-to-control hacker knowledge of a new type of intellectual worker, immaterial labor, vital to a fresh phase of capitalist expansion."[47] This immaterial labor (which of course relies upon other forms of material labor) is particularly important for understanding the labor of videogames.

For the videogames industry, the use and manipulation of information is clearly vital, although it has always been an important part of production. As Manuel Castells noted, "Knowledge and information are critical elements in all modes of development, since the process of production is always based on some level of knowledge and in the processing of information."[48] This phenomenon was noted by the American engineer Frederick Taylor, who, operating from the perspective of capital, developed the theory of scientific management through a series of time and motion studies. Taylor observed that "managers assume . . . the burden of gathering together all of the traditional knowledge which in the past has been possessed by the workmen."[49] Taylor himself carried out this process of knowledge theft—managers stealing from workers—during his experiments at the Midvale Steel Company, where, while working on machine lathes, he tried to understand the labor process from the shop floor.

The importance of information at work therefore predates the rise of contemporary immaterial labor. For Romano Alquati, the importance of information was twofold: first, as "control information," analogous to the knowledge theft of Taylorism outlined above; and second, as information "that constitutes the collective legacy of the working class . . . productive information tout court."[50] This is the kind of information that capital attempts to subsume and transform into the former. This transformation of information into value is a complicated undertaking for capital in the videogame studio.

As I stated earlier, videogames developed from a hacker culture in which developers brought with them the "refusal of work: they signified leisure, hedonism, and irresponsibility against clock punching, discipline, and productivity."[51] Putting this hacker culture to work is a complicated thing for employers because the culture contains this anti-work feeling. This tension creates a contradiction at the heart of the technical composition of labor. Employers attempt to capture the creativity of this subversive culture, but "this capture is not seamless; the capacities that make playbor so productive also make it troublesome."[52] Software development is "at least to a certain extent, a creative and intellectual demanding occupation" and so has to involve a balance between control and autonomy.[53] It is not possible to completely control and regulate the labor processes of software development without stifling the process of production, which means that alternatives and resistance of various kinds need to still find space. The management of immaterial labor involves the need for capital to "balance" its "insatiable need for a stream of innovative ideas with the equally strong imperative to gain control over intellectual property" and workers.[54]

Now that this backdrop to the videogame studio has been sketched, we can identify three factors that shape the workplace.

First, the labor process can be complex and deeply interconnected, without necessarily having clearly defined job descriptions and functions. This can make it difficult to clearly demarcate management and labor, particularly if individuals do not confront each other as buyers and sellers of labor power. Second, in this type of creative work, there may not be stable forms of work with clear boundaries, meaning that traditional notions of the wage-effort bargain may not be effective. Third, the workplace itself may be less defined, without the strict timeframes and distinctions between play and work.[55]

At a basic level, most videogames require some combination of the following roles: designer, who conceives of the game; artist, who creates the visual aspects; programmer, who develops the software of the game, coding and integrating the different parts; level designer, who creates not only the levels of a game but also the challenges and so on; sound engineer, who designs the audio elements of the game, which may include the contributions of voice actors and composers; and tester, who is needed to ensure a game works and its quality is consistent for launch. For an independent developer, these roles might be rolled into one, while for a AAA developer, there may be hundreds of people across these different roles.

The potential of software development is realized under the constraints of capitalist relations of production. This means the kind of software we get is shaped by the way that it is made and under what conditions. Throughout software development history, from the very start, capital has struggled to find effective ways to manage developers. Workers began with a relative position of power and autonomy against capital, but the power relationships have shifted over time. Due to the high demand for software developers early on, many had the freedom to move between jobs and seek comparatively high wages. From the 1970s onward, "many corporate managers . . . were only too eager to impose new technologies and development methodologies that promised to eliminate what they saw as a dangerous dependency on programmer labor," while workers did not create the institutions or structures like labor unions that other professions had.[56] In the context of software development, Philip Kraft has argued that workers were undergoing a process to "break down, simplify, routinise, and standardise" their work in order for it to be completed by "machines rather than people."[57] This claim, made almost forty years ago, explains the ongoing attempts of capital to reduce its reliance on labor in the digital field by driving down the average level of skill required. Similarly, Joan Greenbaum argues that the "design of information systems today is built on a base of previous divisions of labor" inspired by Taylor's scientific management theory.[58]

The application of Taylorism, or at least the standardization of software development in videogames, has involved large-scale investment of capital and intensive division of labor. Within this process, "the creative role of designers and developers faces off against the economic imperatives of efficient production for a competitive market, reflected in the demands of publishers and console manufacturers and embodied in technology."[59] Most videogames are not made from scratch. Instead, developers build upon existing game engines using something called "middleware." This makes "the process of game design easier by offering programmers standardized modules," also known as software development kits (or SDKs).[60] As Graeme Kirkpatrick has noted, the use of technology in the labor process of videogame development involves three related processes. The first is a type of standardization that narrows the creative possibilities for making games. By using the standard packages, there is "a, perhaps imperceptible, effect of inhibiting" programmers' "own ideas about the direction a game might go in, the kinds of event it might include, even its central concept."[61] The second is the use of SDKs to rationalize the labor process, breaking it down into clearer component parts. The use of standardized software components means that the labor process becomes more easily measurable and comparable, opening it up to greater focus and specialization. The third is that SDKs result in a general de-skilling. No longer does a worker need to understand the entire game project; they need to know just one aspect "specified by components with the SDK." This makes it easier to outsource aspects of the game development process too.[62]

The experience of working at these large development studios shows how the production process becomes increasingly complex—mirroring the experiences of workers in many other industries as they have developed. As developer Maxime Beaudoin, who initially believed his "dream came to life" when he was recruited to work on *Assassin's Creed Syndicate*, explained:

> After a few months, Syndicate started for real. The team was getting bigger and bigger as we entered production. For me, this is the root of all issues on AAA games: big teams. Too many people. Syndicate was created with the collaboration of about 10 studios in the world. This is 24-hour non-stop development. When people go to sleep in one studio, it's morning in another one.
>
> With so many people, what naturally occurs is specialization. There's a lot of work to do, and no one can master all the game's systems. So, people specialize, there's no way around it. It can be compared to an assembly line in a car factory. When people realize they're just one very replaceable person on a massive production chain, you can imagine it impacts their motivation.
>
> Being an architect, I had a pretty high level view of all technical developments on the project. While it sounds cool, it has its disadvantages too. The higher you go up the ladder, the less concrete impact you have on the game. You're either a grunt who works on a tiny, tiny part of the game ("See that lamppost? I put it there!"), or you're a high-level director who writes emails and goes to meetings ("See that road full of lampposts? I approved that."). Both positions suck for different reasons. No matter what's your job, you don't have a significant contribution on the game. You're a drop in a glass of water, and as soon as you realize it, your ownership will evaporate in the sun. And without ownership, no motivation.[63]

This account of *Assassin's Creed* reflects a number of key issues already identified by observers of the industry. The first is that videogame production became professionalized—that "firms and workers had 'grown up'" and "moved from the garage to becoming larger, more structured, more managed."[64] For the labor process, this meant that videogame development became more like a "production line," with workers becoming "pigeon-holed" into particular tasks.[65] The result is a more regimented and managed labor process in which workers have lost the creative freedom that they may have had previously. However, management still faces a problem with standardizing work in the studio as "no one project resembles another," with each still having differences.[66]

These kinds of changes were also reflected by another developer, Jean-François Gagné, in his recollection of working on *Assassin's Creed*:

> Basically, I didn't know how to do "anything" anymore. I've worked on six Assassin's Creed games. That was what I was doing since Brotherhood. AC, AC, AC and AC games.... I really knew how to do AC games but that was it! When you are doing the same thing over and over for years ... you forget everything else....
>
> Another thing that is "shocking" on big projects like Syndicate is the layer of managers. From a "floor employee" to the Creative Director you have layers and layers of management, leads, project managers, associate producer, producers, coordinators, production managers, etc. There were also managers to manage managers because they were so many. That was seriously crazy. We had people who were only tracking information between studios. That's what they were doing eight hours a day. Forwarding info from a studio to another. Too many chiefs I must say.[67]

These large-scale projects face the sharpest end of the changes that workers have faced in the labor process—the pressure to meet project deadlines and ensure that significant capital investment goes on to reap profits.

For both Jean-François Gagné and Maxime Beaudoin, their response was looking for another way to make videogames. It should be remembered that this option is available to many workers in the industry, as they are able to act "as purposeful agents, prepared to use the extent of scarcity of skills in the labor market to move on to other companies, sectors (such as IT) or smaller operations."[68] As Beaudoin explained, "For me, going indie also means I can work on non-technical stuff. I like tech, but I also love the creative aspect of games ... gameplay, visuals, sounds, ambiance ... the whole experience. Only indie games will let me cover all aspects of the creation process."[69] Thus the possibility of "going indie" provides the possibility for some workers of escaping these management dynamics. However, this also puts them in a less secure situation as self-employed workers—or owners of small companies—in an incredibly competitive industry.

The managerial control of these larger videogames projects should result in more stable employment, yet the huge scale of videogame development makes projects increasingly harder to manage, resulting in chaotic situations in which jobs are not secure. The story behind the game *Destiny* provides an illustrative example. The development process involved a large team of writers who developed a complex story for the upcoming title. However, after a screening of a "supercut"—a video that covered the key aspects of the story—the senior management decided to scrap the initial version of the story, and instead, with only a year until launch, the studio had to give it a complete overhaul. This led to a bizarre, widely criticized game whose mangled narrative featured a character stating: "I don't have time to explain why I don't have time to explain." Having been reconstructed for management's needs, the storyline bore little resemblance to what those in the studio originally planned. Of course, NDAs have obscured much of this story, but what we do know suggests the ways that strict schedules can create major difficulties in managing the production of videogames.[70] At the start of a typical development process, management sets out "to control, in a highly predictable manner, the outcome of a complex, potentially chaotic production process."[71] The result is often not what is expected or planned for, meaning management comes under increased pressure to meet time-sensitive targets. At the end of projects, this can also mean developers can be sacked, even if they will later be rehired for the next iteration of the project.

In one case, the studio Ready at Dawn finished making *God of War: Ghost of Sparta* and, before moving onto *The Order: 1886*, fired thirteen developers. Six months later they rehired the same positions. The reason for this cyclical sacking is "simple, according to one ex-employee . . . the development team didn't need those people for pre-production—the period of time in which the basics of a game are conceptualised and designed—so Sony, the publisher, wouldn't pay for them."[72] These stories of extreme pressure and scrambling to meet multiple, chaotically managed deadlines are the norm in the development process of videogames.

CRUNCH TIME

Work late, come home, sleep in between stressing about bugs and end up dreaming about code, go back into work and repeat.[73]

The issue of long working hours, known as "crunch time," first came to the fore in 2004. In a now-famous open letter, the wife of a developer at EA (Electronic Arts) explained the realities of this widespread labor practice:

> My significant other works for Electronic Arts, and I'm what you might call a disgruntled spouse.
>
> Our adventures with Electronic Arts began less than a year ago. The small game studio that my partner worked for collapsed as a result of foul play on the part of a big publisher—another common story. Electronic Arts offered a job, the salary was right and the benefits were good, so my S.O. took it. I remember that they asked him in one of the interviews: "How do you feel about working long hours?" It's just a part of the game industry—few studios can avoid a crunch as deadlines loom, so we thought nothing of it. When asked for specifics about what "working long hours" meant, the interviewers coughed and glossed on to the next question; now we know why. . . .

Now, it seems, is the "real" crunch, the one that the producers of this title so wisely prepared their team for by running them into the ground ahead of time. The current mandatory hours are 9am to 10pm–seven days a week–with the occasional Saturday evening off for good behavior (at 6:30pm). This averages out to an eighty-five-hour work week. Complaints that these once more extended hours combined with the team's existing fatigue would result in a greater number of mistakes made and an even greater amount of wasted energy were ignored.

And the kicker: for the honor of this treatment EA salaried employees receive a) no overtime; b) no compensation time! ("comp" time is the equalization of time off for overtime—any hours spent during a crunch accrue into days off after the product has shipped); c) no additional sick or vacation leave. The time just goes away.

The extended hours were deliberate and planned; the management knew what they were doing as they did it. The love of my life comes home late at night complaining of a headache that will not go away and a chronically upset stomach, and my happy supportive smile is running out.

And then if they need to, they hire in a new batch, fresh and ready to hear more promises that will not be kept; EA's turnover rate in engineering is approximately 50 percent. This is how EA works.

If I could get EA CEO Larry Probst on the phone, there are a few things I would ask him. "What's your salary?" would be merely a point of curiosity. The main thing I want to know is, Larry: you do realize what you're doing to your people, right? And you do realize that they ARE people, with physical limits, emotional lives, and families, right? Voices and talents and senses of humor and all that? That when you keep our husbands and wives and children in the office for ninety hours a week, sending them home exhausted and numb and frustrated with their lives, it's not just them you're hurting, but everyone around them, everyone who loves them? When you make your profit calculations and your cost analyses, you know that a great measure of that cost is being paid in raw human dignity, right?[74]

In this personal account of being in a relationship with someone working such long hours, the implications of the practice become starkly clear. The use of NDAs meant that "EA Spouse" had to be anonymous, at first, as a way to reveal the working conditions of her husband. (She was later outed.) However, "very quickly it became clear that the most shocking thing about the EA Spouse story was that, within the industry, it wasn't shocking at all. It was just how things worked."[75] For example, in a survey conducted the same year, it was found that only 2.4 percent of respondents worked in a studio that did not resort to crunch time.[76]

The result of all of this negative publicity caused by the letter was a class action lawsuit over unpaid overtime, which was settled for $15 million. This was then followed by another in 2006, settled for $14.9 million. However, in these settlements, EA "relied on vagaries of American law that classify some IT professionals as exempt from overtime pay. The settlement in the second case featured a quid pro quo: employees would be reclassified in order to get overtime but would give up their stock options."[77] Nonetheless, it appeared at the time like this would be the beginning of the end for the practice of crunching. However, "once the media inevitably lost interest," it did not take much time before "the industry as a whole returned to its culture of inhumanly long hours, too little pay, and high burnout—and remains there today."[78] In fact, since 2004, crunch time has not disappeared from development studios. There has been a general decrease over the past fifteen years, but "crunch time is still part and parcel of the trade." Over half (51 percent) of workers in the IGDA survey reported that they had to work crunch time, which meant putting in "at least 50 percent more hours during crunch than the standard work week of 40 hours." Another 44 percent of workers "reported working long hours or extended hours that they do not refer to as crunch." For either overtime or crunch, 37 percent of workers received no additional compensation. For those who did receive some compensation, it involved perks like food (37 percent) and time off (32 percent), but only 18 percent received additional pay.[79]

Despite these clearly abusive policies, with all the personally devastating costs they incur, crunch time has never even been proven to be an effective managerial strategy. In one study it was found that "no matter how we analyze our data, we find that it loudly and unequivocally supports the anti-crunch side." Not only did the study consider the negative effects for workers; it also demonstrated "that crunch *doesn't* lead to extraordinary results." Furthermore, "on the whole, crunch makes games LESS successful wherever it is used, and when projects try to dig themselves out of a hole by crunching, it only digs the hole deeper."[80] The question, then, is why is the practice so widespread? If you ask the Fryes' friend Karl Marx, the answer is simple: this extension of hours is an attempt to increase the value produced at work.

Marx discusses two ways that surplus value can be gained. The first is through increasing the exploitation of "relative surplus value," which means reducing the amount of labor time needed to produce the equivalent of workers' wages—or getting them to produce more while at work. This can involve new technology or machinery, or the discovery of more efficient ways to organize the workplace. The second way is through increasing "absolute surplus value." This involves extending the productive time at work—making people work longer.[81] Usually, managers choose the first method, as there are social limits (what people are prepared to accept) and natural limits (there are only twenty-four hours in a day) to increasing absolute surplus value.

In view of this framework, it is clear that crunch is therefore a deliberate managerial strategy, not some sort of mistake or aberration. It is one of the major points of contention in the videogames industry. As Tanya Short, the cofounder of an indie studio, explained, "Many teams (indie and AAA alike) seem to start a project *already calculating in* crunch to the schedule for added content or productivity."[82] By consequence of making crunch so prevalent, managers have a skewed understanding of the timing for game development. For example, imagine a designer crunches over three weeks to create a map for a game. Thereafter, a manager will identify a map as taking three weeks and will budget resources for that length of time, even if it should have taken five weeks of "normal" working time. Crunching therefore creates false expectations, particularly when it coincides with a labor process that is difficult to measure or quantify.[83] For Short, "it's absurd. It burns out our most passionate workers. . . . It makes them believe in the martyr syndrome and pushes out all of those voices that literally cannot afford to give away their personal lives."[84] It therefore also become a part of the macho, hardworking ethos that has become widespread in the industry. For example, in 2013 the social media account for a new game, *Ryse*, declared: "By the time #Ryse ships for #XboxOne, we will have served the crunching team more than 11,500 dinners throughout development."[85] What this signals is that managers have not rejected this practice, but rather continue to see it as an integral part of the labor process. Or, as Dyer-Witheford and de Peuter argue, this "normalized crunch time therefore points to an elementary economic fact: it is a good deal—a steal, in fact—for game companies."[86]

SOCIAL COMPOSITION

This utter disregard by the gaming industry for the well-being of its workers brings us to the issue of social composition, the second part of class composition introduced by the editors of *Notes from Below*. "Social composition" refers to the ways in which workers are organized outside of work; it is marked by a broadening of the focus out from the workplace. In a more general sense, it covers aspects like "the conditions of state-provided social services, migration and borders, housing and rent, and a wide range of other issues."[87] The inclusion of the social element represents an attempt to understand how the factors that contribute to the reproduction of labor power (that is, the way in which we recover and prepare for work) also influence the degree to which workers can resist and organize.

To apply this perspective to the videogame industry, it is first necessary to know who composes the workforce. According to the 2017 IGDA survey, a typical worker in the US was likely be a white, straight, nondisabled man, around thirty-five years old, married or in a long-term relationship, and without children.[88] The survey's authors warn that the demographic they describe is "likely overrepresented" in their sample, but is nevertheless a majority in the industry.

A different survey, published in 2015 by the UK-wide organization Creative Skillset, seemed to identify a similar demographic makeup in the UK's videogame workforce. According to the results, most of the workforce consists of young individuals, with 79 percent under the age of thirty-five, and only 4.7 percent representation for Black and minority ethnic (BAME) workers. Only 14 percent identify as women—who also earn on average 15 percent less than men.[89] Yet another survey found that 45 percent "felt that their gender had been a limiting factor in their career progression, offering a significant barrier to their progress. A further 33 percent said that they had experienced direct harassment or bullying because of their gender."[90] This shocking set of statistics highlights the importance of considering gender, not only within videogames, but also in the workplace itself.

The managerial practices of crunch feed directly into this issue, with the "long-hours culture" acting as both a cause and effect of the institutionalized sexism in the industry.[91] Those with caring responsibilities, who are overwhelmingly women, find it harder to work such long days, which means this kind of work can become off limits for them. They therefore face direct barriers that are the result of sexism. These take the form of a "glass ceiling" preventing career progression, but also as additional pressures in terms of the "classic invisible role of reproductive labor, covering the deficit of household tasks and emotional labor of which [women's] exhausted partners are incapable."[92]

Regarding the lack of diversity, the 2017 IGDA survey sug-
gested that it is less a concern for people hiring workers than it is
for the workers themselves. The question of "whether or not diversity was important" generated the highest number of responses in
the history of the survey: 81 percent felt it was "very important"
or "somewhat important."[93] In part, this sentiment comes from
the experiences that workers have in the workplace, through bias
they perceived either toward themselves or others. A majority
(56 percent) had "perceived inequity towards" themselves "on the
basis of gender, age, ethnicity, ability, or sexual persuasion," and
a minority (44 percent) had perceived inequity toward others.
This included inequity in relation to issues of recruitment, hiring,
promotion, salary and other forms of compensation, disciplinary
action, interpersonal relations, microaggressions, workload, and
working conditions. Only around half of workers were employed
in companies that had a policy advancing equity or diversity,
such as a "general non-discrimination policy" (57 percent), an
"equal opportunity hiring policy" (49 percent), or a "sexual harassment policy" (48 percent). Within that group, only 26 percent
had a "formal complaint procedure," and only 21 percent had
any "formal disciplinary process" regarding such policies. As a
result of this lack of accountability, only a little more than half of
workers (56 percent) believed that these "policies were adequately
enforced," and 50 percent of respondents thought that "there is
equal treatment and opportunity for all in the game industry";
another 17 percent were not sure there is equal treatment.

These kinds of views can also be understood in light of the
mixed opinions of how society sees the industry in general.
Overall, workers in the industry were divided: "38% felt that society has a negative view, 37% felt that society has a positive
view, and 25% felt that there is a neutral view."[94] Respondents
identified factors they thought contributed to the negative view
that large segments have of the industry: sexism among gamers
(57 percent), sexism in games (55 percent), perceived link to violence (55 percent), working conditions (54 percent), perceived
link to obesity (46 percent), racism among gamers (40 percent),

sexism in the workforce (39 percent), lack of overall diversity (38 percent), racism in games (24 percent), racism in the workforce (17 percent), other (12 percent), and "I don't think there is a negative perception of the games industry" (7 percent).[95]

Social composition is concerned with how the worker is composed outside of the labor process and technical composition of work. Looking at these social factors beyond the workplace is key to making sense of the workplace itself. For example, the fact that the composition of the workforce is most likely young and male, without family-care responsibilities, makes the widespread use of "crunch time" possible. Either the workers have no family-care responsibilities, or they can shift them onto their partners—or outsource it to paid care workers. This creates a gendered division of labor that follows the broader dynamics of society, with development work coded as a male form of work and caring a female one.

The mobilization of passion around videogame culture—something that begins in the consumption, rather than the production, of videogames—is another important social factor that shapes the videogames workplace from the outside. As I discussed earlier, videogame work is associated with play in two ways: both with the game that is the outcome of the work, but also with the hacker ethos of the early videogame era, the work-as-play philosophy of companies like Atari, as well as an impassioned feeling among workers of being a part of something. In broad terms, this means that the "people who work in the games industry are, invariably, invested in gaming as a cultural practice," and therefore "games are made by gamers, with all that implies."[96]

Working within a culture driven by passion has significant implications. For example, "geek culture," often associated with the videogames community, involves people taking "such strongly held commonalities of interest and consumption far more seriously than most other subcultures." This culture is used against workers, particularly in the videogames industry. As Ian Williams explains, "Capital harnesses geek culture to actively harm workers."[97] The high level of "prestige" that workers attain "means that many who work in the industry are prepared to work long hours, sometimes unpaid, and to put up with precarious terms of employment."[98]

Without taking into account social composition, it is not possible to understand the leap from how work is organized by capital to how workers can resist and organize. Another challenge with videogame workers—and a particular obstacle in their organizing efforts—is understanding how this comparatively small segment of workers relates to other workers in the industry more generally. While they work in the same industry, videogame workers often do not share workplaces with workers involved in publishing and retail. It is also useful here to recognize the differences between videogame workers and software developers in other industries. As discussed before, videogame workers receive comparatively high wages and can be difficult to manage, often due to their specialist knowledge and skills. These workers are relatively powerful, particularly compared with the others along the value chain that we discussed above. Two key mobilizing factors—crunch time and equality—are provoking a process of political recomposition through which workers are beginning to express this power.

ORGANIZING IN THE
VIDEOGAMES INDUSTRY

When I first thought about writing this book, I planned this chapter as a discussion of how and why workers in the videogames industry might organize. I sketched out how examples could be used from the struggles of the Screen Actors Guild and American Federation of Television and Radio Artists in the 1920 and '30s (which later merged into SAG-AFTRA) as well as other initiatives like WashTech (Washington Alliance of Technology Workers). However, as I started to write the book, a process of political recomposition began to unfold in the tech industry, which meant imagining the possibilities was no longer necessary because organizing was becoming a reality.

Tech Workers Coalition is one example of this process. TWC is a "coalition of workers in and around the tech industry, labor organizers, community organizers, and friends" that is based in the US, and particularly active in the Bay Area and Seattle.[1] In the past few years, the network has gone from strength to strength. As R. K. Upadhya, a member of TWC, explained: "Since the 2016 elections in the US, there has been an unprecedented level of visible unrest among workers at all levels in the tech industry, from food service workers to programmers and engineers."[2] For TWC, this unrest has led to tech workers organizing, but it has also spawned cross-sector campaigns at the so-called campus workplaces, with tech workers—who often enjoy better pay, terms, and conditions—supporting the struggles of other groups of service workers. As Jason Prado, a software developer, wrote in an article published in *Notes from Below*: "Service workers on my company's campuses have organized and won union contracts, and workers further up the hierarchy have actively supported these efforts." Through circulating petitions, going to meetings, and taking part in actions, the groups are forming a reciprocal relationship. The "service workers and professional union organizers," Prado said, "are happy to leverage support from high-prestige tech employees, and tech employees gain firsthand experience working on an organizing campaign." This kind of connection has been rare in the past. But "workers from different roles quickly come to identify together when engaged in struggle. Said another way, no comrade in an actual struggle has stopped to ask, 'Are tech workers really working-class?' Solidarity is built in struggle."[3]

TWC has grown into a kind of focal point, collecting together and generalizing different struggles in the tech industry. As Upadhya explained, "There has been a lot of spontaneous organizing and unrest happening in the industry in the past couple of years, but still the key task right now for us is to start with the basics of agitation and organizing. This is where 'workers' inquiry' comes in."[4] Members of TWC began using an approach inspired by workers' inquiry, getting people together to talk about problems at work and ways to organize. As a TWC representative explained in a presentation in Toronto in 2018:

> Our premise is that getting workers to talk to each other about problems that they have in the workplace is a powerful way to agitate, and build toward organizing; and that for would-be organizers like the core of TWC, there is no way in hell that you can have an effective campaign if you don't know what your coworkers are actually thinking about and care about. It's also an effective way to better understand what we can call the "class composition" of the tech industry; or in other words, where are people coming from in terms of backgrounds and occupations, where are they specifically

located in the industry, what supply chains they're a part of, and so on.[5]

This is an example of organic organizing that has taken up the idea of workers' inquiry and refreshed it for use under new conditions. It involves workers drawing in part from older forms, but also finding new ways to resist and struggle. Despite the projections by many outside the tech industry that organizing was a long way off, workers themselves found new ways to mobilize, and workers' inquiry played a facilitating role.

These struggles in the tech industry have not directly fed into the videogames industry. However, they do form part of the backdrop behind a similar moment involving videogame workers. In 2016, voice actors within the US videogames industry went on strike. These workers, who were part of the SAG-AFTRA union, targeted their strike against eleven major companies, including EA and Activision. There were four main demands. First, the union wanted bonuses based on sales, a demand that addressed the fact that videogame contracts did not include secondary compensation, unlike with other SAG-AFTRA contracts. Second, the actors demanded greater transparency from companies, including that actors are informed what a project entails before it begins. Third, the union demanded that workers' concerns be taken seriously, particularly in relation to vocal stress and safety. Fourth, the union demanded an updated contract, as the existing one was negotiated in 1994.[6] When the negotiations started, the lawyer representing the studios (as quoted by a voice actor who observed the meetings) started off by saying: "It's so great to see so many of you coming here to support your contract, we're very proud to see you all here. Really no one cares about voiceover in video games, and we could get anyone to do what you do for 50 bucks an hour. So we're showing extraordinary good faith by even turning up."[7]

Voice acting is a difficult and stressful role, particularly in videogames, in which actors are expected to record extreme performances. As one voice actor explained, "Look, I get it: from their end, it's an engine and a set of algorithms that perform certain functions. The trouble is that voice acting doesn't just slot in like a stick of RAM."[8] These workers were treated as being external to the industry, despite the key role that audio plays in many games. The strike itself lasted over a year, ending with the parties reaching a deal. While it did not meet all of their demands, it nevertheless had a broader impact across the industry.[9] It also stirred up some controversy. One of the points of contention, as writer and developer Dante Douglas explained, was in regard to secondary compensation: "If voice actors received royalties before developers, it would be unfair to those who worked on parts of the game other than voice acting, and that they deserved bonuses and/or royalties as well." This argument was centered on the fact that "there was no organization behind developers that had the bargaining strength of SAG-AFTRA." However, soon after the settlement, things would begin to change.[10]

On February 14, twenty-one workers went on strike at Eugen Systems, a French videogames studio. Their statement, released through Le Syndicat des Travailleurs et Travailleuses du Jeu Vidéo (STJV, the videogame workers union), read, "In the face of the refusal to pay us as required by law, and the manifest lack of consideration for the value of our work, we have come to the conclusion that, in order to make ourselves heard, we have no option but to go on strike."[11] The roots of the strike lay in one developer looking closely at existing labor contracts and coming across the SYNTEC collective bargaining agreement, which covered tech workers generally and therefore included videogame workers.[12] Along with employee terms over pay and overtime compensation, this agreement also included the workers' "right to log-off," and not be required to answer emails after 6 p.m. Discovering that these terms applied to them, the workers attempted to negotiate with management about their concerns.[13] These peculiarities of the French industrial relations system, along with the formation of the union in the autumn of 2017, provided the channel for this action. However, the concerns of the French workers are also shared by game workers in many different countries, and thus show how these grievances can be turned into organizing.

After thirty days on strike, one of the activists, Félix Habert, reflected on their experience by that point: "It's rather hard when you're just a bunch of people with no political experience."[14] However, they had also discovered mistakes in how the company organized payments, crowdfunded ten thousand dollars in strike funds, and made international news with their campaign. As one journalist reflected at the time, "It's a small but symbolic labor dispute in one of the country's most often praised economic sectors that could have ramifications for workers at other studios."[15] The strike, which Habert described as "a very spontaneous movement," ended in the second week of April, even though the strikers' demands were not met. Some then chose to take legal action against the studio.[16] The STJV has continued to build from this strike, representing not only workers in the industry, but also students and unemployed workers. The union has since focused on campaigns against unpaid internships, low wages for starting workers, and precarious contracts.[17]

These initial struggles of voice actors in the US and videogame workers in France foreshadowed the emergence of a new organization. This is not to say that videogame workers in studios across the world have been passive—rather, that these were some of the few open moments of class struggle. Nevertheless, there are likely to have been countless moments of less publicized resistance from frustrated or angry workers in studios across the world, the overwhelming majority of which would never have made the news.

The next stage of the workers' recomposition had a flashpoint on March 21, 2018. The Game Developers Conference (GDC)—the world's largest professional games industry event, hosted in San Francisco—had scheduled a roundtable discussion titled "Union Now? Pros, Cons, and Consequences of Unionization for Game Devs." The discussion was to be hosted by Jen MacLean, who had recently been appointed the executive director of the IGDA, an organization considered hostile to unionization. In an interview a few days before, MacLean had claimed that regarding the problem of job losses, "a union's not going to change that, access to capital is going to change that," demonstrating quite clearly which side she was on.[18] As Ian Williams has argued, while there were some "token board appointments" for the IGDA to appease developers and similar groups, these were intended to "hide the organization's true purpose of blunting any *real* change which could possibly be affected by workers."[19]

In response to these developments, videogame workers started to discuss a possible intervention. "[One] small Facebook group became a bigger one on Twitter, which then became an even bigger movement across multiple channels ... and suddenly a direct action was in place."[20] They planned to turn up to the roundtable, making sure it was packed with pro-union voices. Workers from across the industry began engaging in "an enthusiastic virtual salon, talking tactics, strategy, and theory to figure out how" to "get from what was and is to what can be."[21] Scott Benson, the cocreator of the fantastic indie game *Night in the Woods*, created a logo for the group. The logo and the name Game Workers Unite (GWU) was added to a new website as well as to leaflets and badges. However, as Williams points out, "annoyance, even fury, doesn't mean much if it's not translated to action on the ground. Aesthetics don't win rights."[22]

By the time GDC came around, the stage was set for a showdown. Jen MacLean introduced the roundtable session on unionization, stressing that the meeting should have a tone of respectability and congeniality.[23] There were two outside speakers, both representatives from the International Alliance of Theatrical Stage Employees union. However, as the meeting progressed, and more pro-union voices began to speak out, the "tone of respectability and politeness had been revealed for an excuse to tone police and shut down conversation, to manipulate speakers." As Michelle Ehrhardt reported, the IGDA tried to "misrepresent what unions do and prevent any organizing that had been taking place that day from taking root." She also noted that "MacLean's tactics of silencing, leading and derailing just as

speakers were about to discuss organizing could be seen as purposeful union-busting." After all, the IGDA is not only ideologically but also practically hostile to the emergence of grassroots
organizing, and thus is "threatened by the existence of an actual
union that may usurp it."[24]

The leaflet—or zine, as some referred to it—that was handed
out at the meeting is a great example of how videogame culture
can be effectively merged with pro-union propaganda. As was
explained when it was reposted on *Notes from Below*, the "zine
provides a much needed starting point for organising workers—
many of whom have no experience with trade unions previously.
It is an accessible introduction, explaining why a union is needed,
along with practical steps for organising."[25] The full-color zine
is presented like a videogame magazine. The cover page features the Sonic the Hedgehog character with a microphone,
surrounded by text: "Stay Alive in the Industrial Zone!" "Tips
for Beating All the Bosses," "Co-op Tactics," and "Free Strategy
Guide Inside!" The first page lays out the program: "Hey you!
Are you tired of crunch? Worried management isn't listening to
your concerns? Are you struggling to pay bills, or lacking basic
benefits like health care insurance or paid parental leave? Do you
suspect you're being paid less than your co-workers because of
your race or gender?" Accompanying these questions is the logo
of Game Workers Unite—a raised fist holding a game controller.
The subsequent page lays out the official platform of GWU:

> Game Workers Unite is a broad-reaching organization that
> seeks to connect pro-union activists, exploited workers, and al-
> lies across borders and across ideologies in the name of build-
> ing a unionized game industry. We are building pro-union
> solidarity across disciplines, classes, and countries. The organ-
> ization is run exclusively by workers (non-employers), but we
> actively encourage employers, academics, and others to engage
> in the community and help support the organization's direct
> action efforts both materially and through their visibility.[26]

This is followed by a takedown of the anti-union IGDA that is
in the style of a game review with scores. A longer "cover feature"

then explains in an accessible manner what a union is and why people should join. This is the "strategy guide" promised on the cover:

> What are some concrete steps I can take towards unionizing? If you work in the game industry, the first step is to talk with fellow workers outside of your employer's supervision, starting with the people you trust. Talk to them about your working conditions, ask them what their concerns are, and if they aren't already informed, share info about unions *(like this mag! -ed.)* You should also contact existing local unions to seek their help and advice on how to unionize your workplace. Make sure to keep discussions about the possibility of unionizing away from the ears of employers, even if you think they're sympathetic to your cause![27]

Throughout its pages the zine employs a tongue-in-cheek sense of humor, pitching concepts in terms that people in the industry would be familiar with but without losing the politics of organizing. The zine has been shared widely beyond the initial meeting, with multiple sites hosting the pdf file and updating it with local contact details. It also shows the preparatory work that had been put into the intervention at GDC.

As Emma (who uses a pseudonym), an organizer for GWU, stated in an interview, the event at GDC was a key starting point. From this meeting, they established three points of action for GWU. The first was the formation of local chapters. A few months after the meeting, there were local chapters in the US, Canada, Germany, United Kingdom, Brazil, and Australia, with many more in the process of formation. Emma explained that they "really believe in distributed organizing, and giving the tools and connections and power to people on a local scale, to work within their communities and actually build real solidarity and unionization efforts there."[28] The second step was doing "educational campaigning," particularly on behalf of unions—not only with a focus on "anti-union myth-busting" but also relating to what worker's "legal rights are, in terms of fighting for a better workplace . . . the actual steps of unionizing." The third was working with existing unions and other organizations to work out how to move GWU forward, forming alliances and sharing tactics. Unsurprisingly, in the US this has involved working with SAG-AFTRA and drawing on experiences from STJV in France. However, the scale of the fight that GWU is starting is certainly not insignificant. Emma summed it up as being "very 'David and Goliath.' That's kind of the nature of the fight."[29]

GWU is still in an early stage at the time of writing this book (and with each successive draft, much has changed). Following in the footsteps of previous workers' inquiries, my response upon finding out about the GDC event and zine was to immediately get in contact with GWU. Through Twitter, I was directed first to the national organization, then to the local chapter in the UK. (So far, I have been participating in the early stages of organizing, offering advice and support.) I got in touch with one of the lead organizers in the UK, Declan (who often goes by the nickname "Dec" and, like the other organizers, will only be referred to by first name). Like me, he first saw the zine handed out at GDC, so, he explained, "I went to their website and I read it and was like I'm really, really interested in unionisation."[30] Both of Dec's parents were trade unionists, so he had some prior experience, albeit in very different industries. From that first introduction with the international GWU, Dec started GWU UK, starting up a server on Discord (a voice and text chat application popular with videogame players) to bring people together. He explained what he saw as the source of GWU's growth:

> The industry is just at that point where, not just the games industry, it's like politics in general, we've got to that point where sort of left ideas, unions and whatnot, people are actually questioning: "Hey, why are people not in unions anymore? Why is the tech industry and Silicon Valley not built like other industries where there are actual protections for workers?" I think everything built up with people asking these questions and I think someone finally just took the initiative. As soon as someone did, everyone jumped on it, because I think everyone who is involved right now has just

been expecting some people to start it, and then they can jump on it. I know I was. It's that critical point.[31]

There have been significant changes in the industry, and Dec, a relatively new entrant, has felt them particularly. He discussed how some of what he did was closer to "gig work" and that employers take advantage of workers' "passion" for working on videogames. Dec identified two key reasons for unionizing in the UK videogames industry:

> Crunch. The process in the games industry with employers just saying so we're a month away from the end of the project—well three months actually—everyone has to work overtime, it's in your contract that you have to do it unpaid.... How like on average people like go into the game industry for about three years and then leave because they realise that this is the case. That they are basically being had by employers, because everyone wants to work on games and employers know that and so they burn them out and then bring in someone else. So yeah, it's like burnout ... that and gender representation and racial representation.... It's still really bad in the games industry.[32]

These two issues, crunch and representation, form a powerful set of grievances from which workers can organize and struggle. On the question of where GWU may go in the UK, Dec drew on traditional concepts from trade unions, updating them for a new context. He argued that "negotiating for contracts" was a start, but it was also important to organize in AAA studios and "to encourage indie developers to say: 'We're a union studio.'" However, he recognized that this was not something that employers were likely to do willingly. One strategic response that Dec outlined for developers started directly from the work process:

> In game development everyone is constantly interacting with everyone else and if suddenly you had nobody to talk about with for design decisions, or nobody to give you new art assets, or nobody to do any of the code, in any of those situations you would stop, everything stops. So, it's like an assembly line, it's like a huge network. With my job, with just ten

people, I'm interacting with all of the programmers and all of the artists every day. I wouldn't be able to do my job without them. If the artists went on strike it would bring the entire studio to a halt. We, the designers and the coders, would just have to make cubes.[33]

Despite the novelty of the new kinds of work in videogame studios, Dec is confident that strike action could still be used as a weapon. For example, in Dec's hypothetical strike, the production of a videogame could grind to a stop if only a few people went on strike. However, it would only make sense for workers to strike once the project was already underway and their work had become crucial for ongoing development; otherwise, they would risk simply being laid off. As with the TWC example, this has to begin from not only understanding the labor process but also the ways workers relate to the projects.

As I have written elsewhere, these workers are meeting, discussing, and experimenting with what a union would mean in their own context.[34] For example, at their first national meeting, the importance of videogame culture became clear. Most of the workers who arrived were clearly identifiable by their videogame-themed T-shirts—as well as the Nintendo-themed trainers and *World of Warcraft* "Horde"-themed leggings. Most noteworthy was that while no one at the meeting had ever been in a trade union before—or were that clear on what it would entail—they all wanted to start one. Many were under the impression that you had to tell your employer if you joined a union (this is not required in the UK), which made their decision to start organizing even more brave. At the end of the meeting, one worker approached me. He was keen to join the union but wanted to know whether he would have to talk to other workers in the studio about it. After I explained that would probably be a good idea, he replied, "Fuck, that's really scary!" We discussed at length how to gradually build up to talking about organizing at work, including organizer training and role-playing. He went away from the meeting having resolved that he could handle the challenge. What these early conversations show is that the new members of GWU are not merely interested in joining a union; they are already oriented toward organizing at work—something that many established unions could learn from.

At each of the GWU meetings in London, what can be seen is this process of recomposition in action. The UK branch is now the first to form a trade union. They began discussions with a range of different trade unions in the UK, and settled on joining the Independent Workers Union of Great Britain, or IWGB. In my previous research, I have worked with members of this union in workers' inquiry projects as well as organizing (and also as a member).[35] This small union started by organizing with cleaners, porters, security guards, and other university workers; then it moved on to organize foster care workers, Uber drivers, bicycle couriers, Deliveroo riders, and electricians. While videogame workers may sound like an unusual addition to this lineup, what unites these groups of workers is that they have been left out of the organizing efforts of mainstream trade unions or have been considered unorganizable.

At this writing, GWU looks to be the most exciting experiment for organizing workers in the videogame industry. Its success is not guaranteed, but the method of workers' inquiry provides a powerful way to understand the tendency of struggles as they spread through these previously unorganized workplaces. It also points toward the possibility of a very different kind of videogames industry from what we have discussed so far.

PART II

PLAYING VIDEOGAMES

ANALYZING CULTURE

I recently experienced The Void's *Star Wars: Secrets of the Empire*, a virtual reality (VR) game, in a shopping center in London. This was an encounter radically different from my earliest memories with those old MS-DOS games and their tiny computer monitors. First off, the experience cost almost as much as a videogame for a console. Upon arrival at the venue, we checked our bags and the bored-looking teenager behind the desk asked us—in a flat tone—if we were "ready for our mission." We were then asked to watch a live-action introduction to the game, delivered by one of the film's actors. The scenario has you, a rebel fighter, going undercover as a stormtrooper to infiltrate a base and discover the contents of a mysterious box. The weight of the portable VR gear that you strap into works in this context—only a little bit cumbersome, the gear gives the sense of wearing armor. When the game begins, you walk through a door into a real-life setting—actual walls and doors that the game is mapped onto.

My first instinct was to hold up my hands, and the hands of a stormtrooper appeared. My partner also held her hands up, and we stood in awe. The sense of scale was astonishing as we stepped through into another room and now stood on a moving platform above a virtual planet with lava below us. Heat was generated in our real-world room, adding to the immersion in a way I only thought about later. The combination of VR and real-world details offered a genuinely impressive sense of interactivity. The game itself combined shooting, puzzle solving, and simply taking in the surroundings. In this moment of cinematic immersion, I kept thinking back to what the child version of me would make of the experience. It was then over, far too quickly, and we were ejected back into the loud, fluorescent, and air-conditioned surroundings of the shopping center. Clearly, there have been big changes since those days of MS-DOS and floppy disks.

In order to make sense of these changes, it is useful to explore and critique some contemporary videogames. It would be impossible to cover the full spectrum of games available since that would involve approximately eighty-three games.[1] But before diving into some of those games, we should reflect on why it even matters to analyze and critique videogames in the first place, or culture in general, for that matter.

Investigating how videogames are played is clearly different from understanding how they are made. Yes, the production and distribution process shapes the kinds of games we play and how we play them. Yet, so far in this book I have paid less attention to the actual finished commodity itself. Now we turn to discuss videogames themselves.

Nick Dyer-Witheford and Greig de Peuter argue:

> Just as the eighteenth-century novel was a textual apparatus generating the bourgeois personality required by mercantile colonialism (but also capable of criticizing it), and just as twentieth-century cinema and television were integral to industrial consumerism (yet screened some of its darkest depictions), so virtual games are constitutive of twenty-first-century global hypercapitalism and, perhaps, also of lines of exodus from it.[2]

Therefore, by looking at the videogames that are being made and played today, it is possible to make a broader argument about the medium. For me, this interest unfolded in a similar way to how Ernest Mandel, connecting crime fiction and Marxism, wrote the book *Delightful Murder: A Social History of the Crime Story*:

> Let me confess at the outset that I like to read crime stories. I used to think that they were simply escapist entertainment: when you read them, you don't think about anything else;

when you finish one, you don't think about it again. But this little book is itself proof that this way of looking at it is at least incomplete. True enough, once you finish any particular crime novel, you stop being fascinated by it; but equally, I, for one, cannot help being fascinated by the enormous success of the crime story as a literary genre.[3]

As with Mandel reading crime fiction, I also like to play videogames (something I hope has become clear already!). While I do not think that the experience of videogames leaves us as quickly as reading a crime book, I too want to understand how videogames work, beyond just playing them. I too think Marxism can help us understand different mass forms of culture. Mandel's claim in the preface to *Delightful Murder* still rings true:

> To those who consider it frivolous for a Marxist to spend time analyzing crime stories, I can only offer this final apology: historical materialism can—and should—be applied to all social phenomenon. None is by nature less worthy of study than others. The majesty of this theory—and the proof of its validity—lies precisely in its ability to explain them all.[4]

The application of Marxism to the play of videogames can take important inspiration from the Marxist cultural theorist Raymond Williams. In his 1974 book *Television*, Williams lays out an approach for analyzing mass forms of culture that we can continue from. He begins by noting that "it is often said that television has altered our world. In the same way, people often speak of a new world, a new society, a new phase of history, being created—'brought about'—by this or that new technology."[5] The book explores the television as a technology and as a cultural form. The focus on both is important. If television—or indeed videogames—is treated as the cause of change, then "we can at best modify or seek to control its effects." On the other hand, "if the technology, as used, is an effect, to what other kinds of cause, and other kinds of action, should we refer and relate our experience of its uses?"[6] If we apply this logic, we should therefore think of videogames as a technology that comes out of the conditions of existing society. Videogames, then, are played within those conditions, both shaping what kind of games we can play as well as how we play them.

We can apply Williams's approach to understand videogames in a number of ways: by thinking of them as a "technology," as "work," as part of contemporary capitalism, and as a cultural form of "play." So while we are talking about videogames, we are also talking about a lot more than videogames. Too often, when videogames are subjected to critique, the focus echoes something that Williams previously noted with television. Much attention was focused on "sex" and "violence," as well as "political manipulation" and "cultural degradation." This has been the case with videogames too—particularly with respect to "violence" and "cultural degradation"—which highlights something not specific to the form of either television or videogames (or indeed the novel or comics). The reason this is the case, Williams explains, is that "the effect [is] seen as an ideology: a way of interpreting general change through a displaced and abstracted cause."[7]

As it turns out, Marx and Marxism can provide tools for the cultural criticism of videogames. However, this may seem like a somewhat odd thing to say since Marxism is, after all, a theory of revolution. As Marx and Engels argued, "Communism is for us not a *state of affairs* which is to be established, an *ideal* to which reality [will] have to adjust itself. We call communism the *real* movement which abolishes the present state of things."[8]

Marxism is therefore a theory and a practice that aims at the revolutionary overthrow of capitalism. However, as Marx and Engels note, "the conditions of this movement result from the premises now in existence." While the conditions of work, the relationship between classes, the productive forces, and so on are crucial to a Marxist perspective, society is also composed of more than just economic relations. This is of course not to say that the cultural dimensions of videogames are as important as the relationships of exploitation required for their production, but rather that they are also worth examining for their ideological content. With regard to ideology, Marx and Engels explain:

> The production of ideas, concepts and consciousness is first of all directly interwoven with the material intercourse of man, the language of real life. Conceiving, thinking, the spiritual intercourse of men, appear here as the direct efflux of men's material behaviour.... We do not proceed from what men say, imagine, conceive, nor from men as described, thought of, imagined, conceived, in order to arrive at corporeal man; rather we proceed from the really active man ... consciousness does not determine life: life determines consciousness.[9]

Furthermore, according to Marx:

> In the social production of their life, men enter into definite relations that are indispensable and independent of their will, relations of production which correspond to a definite stage of development of their material productive forces. The sum total of these relations of production constitutes the economic structure of society, the real foundation, on which rises a legal and political superstructure and to which correspond definite forms of social consciousness. The mode of production of material life conditions the social, political and intellectual life process in general. It is not the consciousness of men that determines their being, but on the contrary, their social being that determines their consciousness.[10]

Videogames arise from this material base, to use this often-mentioned, rarely fully quoted, and even more rarely understood metaphor of the base or superstructure. The specific economic relations of production that we have discussed therefore shape the kinds of hardware, software, and videogames that can be and are produced. However, this is not a one-way process, nor does economics entirely determine the superstructure.

To make sense of this relationship with videogames, we can draw upon a long history of Marxist readings of culture. As Terry Eagleton notes, however, the relevance of a Marxist reading of culture to revolutionary struggle "is not immediately apparent." Nevertheless, he goes on to argue that Marxist criticism is important because it is "part of a larger body of theoretical analysis which aims to understand *ideologies*—the ideas, values and feelings by which men experience their societies at various times." A Marxist critique of literature, and indeed of videogames, is part of a project to understand ideologies: to "understand both the past and the present more deeply; and such understanding contributes to our liberation."[11] After all, when Marx was living in Brussels (before he penned the call for a workers' inquiry), he founded a German workers' circle that spent one evening each week discussing arts and culture.[12]

The links between the economic relations—that the workers in the circle were subjected to—and the cultural or artistic aspects they were discussing are different in important ways. The economic base of society is constituted by relations and forces of production. Stemming from these, but also going beyond, are the superstructural elements that Marx discusses. These are composed of "definite forms of social consciousness (political, religious, ethical, aesthetic and so on)," which together form "ideology," as discussed above. Ideology should receive our focus because its function is "to legitimate the power of the ruling class in society; in the last analysis, the dominant ideas of society are the ideas of its ruling class."[13] The challenge here is that ideology is not a straightforward or direct command to obey—it is a far more complex, subtle, obscured, and even contradictory phenomenon than that.

Both Marx and Engels discussed how the relationship between base and superstructure was far from straightforward. Engels argued:

> According to the materialist conception of history, the determining element of history is *ultimately* the production and reproduction in real life. More than this neither Marx nor I have ever asserted. If therefore somebody twists this statement that the economic element is the *only* determining one, he transforms it into a meaningless, abstract and absurd phrase. The economic situation is the basis, but the various elements of the superstructure—political forms of the class struggle and its consequences, constitutions established by the victorious class after a successful battle, etc . . . also exercise their influ-

ence upon the course of the historical struggles and in many cases preponderate in determining their *form*.[14]

The argument here is not only that you can draw a direct line from the base to the superstructure, but that the ideological superstructure also reflects back upon the economic base. As Eagleton reiterates, elements of the superstructure "are not reducible to a mere expression of the class struggle or the state of the economy."[15] Yet, Marxism also asserts that "in the last analysis, art is determined by that mode of production."[16] What Eagleton calls this "apparent discrepancy" is important to bear in mind when thinking about cultural commodities. It makes sense to understand how the commodity came out of economic relations, but also to understand it as a cultural artifact. This is also why we should try to understand videogames through workers' inquiry and class composition: ultimately, these relations of production are key to understanding the form.

Videogames are not just made, they are made to be *played*. So now we will turn to discuss the active engagement with videogames that comes through playing them, going beyond how they are made to reach an understanding of the final product.

FIRST-PERSON SHOOTERS

The genre of the first-person shooter (or FPS) videogame offers, as the name suggests, a first-person perspective to players, and the aim of the game involves shooting things—usually representations of people. With their instantly recognizable viewpoint, these are the kinds of games that many people think of when they think of videogames. While FPS games are not the only ones that deal with the subject of war—there are also simulations and strategy games of various kinds—they deal with it from the visceral perspective of a direct participant. There are also variants of FPS games that take on different angles, science fiction settings, and so on, but they are at their core still about armed conflict. These kinds of videogames have been critiqued for, among other reasons, glorifying military conflict and desensitizing violence—and have often been the target of negative press. FPS videogames set in the past engage with the production of history—whether imagined or with a varying degree of connection to historical events—and therefore entail a link with memories of conflicts or violence. As Nina Huntemann has noted, "video games tell stories," and the "fact that war video games sell so well, tells us these stories are compelling to many millions of people."[1] Therefore, it is important to unpack the kinds of stories that are being told in these games.

The FPS videogame allows players to get close to the action—you see the same view you would imagine someone would in a real scenario—while providing a tactile interaction to go with it. Here we can understand FPS as one of the consequences stemming from the pivotal shift from stage acting to screen acting, as noted by cultural critic Walter Benjamin. The screen actor's "performance is mediated by the camera," and therefore "deprived of the possibility open to the stage actor of adapting that performance to the audience as the show goes on; the cinema audience is being asked to examine and report without any personal contact with the performer intruding." The FPS perspective is a further alteration of this pivotal shift. No longer does the audience (reduced from the multiple view to the singular) interact through "the camera's stance"; this stance itself becomes part of the interaction—with the player able to choose how to explore and interact with the scene.[2] This is not a direct comparison, but the fact that this genre allows people to have the experience of "'getting close to things' in both spatial and human terms" demonstrates its affinity with what Walter Benjamin found in mass-produced art.[3]

The closeness of the first-person perspective is important. However, the success of FPS games is "not simply the first-person perspective, the three-dimensionality, the violence, or the escape," but rather how these are combined "in a distinct way: a virtual environment that maximizes a player's potential to attain a state that the psychologist Mihaly Csikszentmihalyi calls 'flow.'"[4] For Csikszentmihalyi, "flow" is the feeling of immersion, presence, and happiness—or more colloquially, of being "in the zone."[5] Andrew Feenberg, in his observations of players of the Japanese game Go, refers to this kind of experience as "no-mind," calling it a spiritual phenomenon.[6] The aesthetic transformation noted of fighting videogames—and this holds for FPS as well—has resulted in a type of "flow" that "enables the most skilled play but also the most profound experience of play."[7] In the case of FPS games, this becomes "self-reinforcing," with a compulsion to return to the game.[8] This powerful feedback loop has drawn in huge audiences to play FPS games, often for extended periods of time. Any player of videogames has likely felt this—something pulls us into a videogame. It is an experience that is much more rarely found with other forms of contemporary culture.

FPS games have a long history. Arguably the first modern FPS was *Wolfenstein 3D*, released in 1992. Featuring B. J. Blazkowicz as the player's avatar, "a Caucasian male, with a military background," the game set "the foundation of the First-Person Shooter (FPS) genre.... There were earlier ancestors, but *Wolfenstein 3D* certainly played a large role in the style's growth."[9] Although the plot of the game focuses on a single American spy defeating huge numbers of Nazi soldiers, it does not stick that closely to historical details. It features a Nazi plan to raise an army of undead mutants, and Hitler, augmented with a mechanical suit and quad chain guns. The basic elements of FPS gameplay were laid down at this stage: the player views the world, and "looking and targeting came together in the same movement, and the player was invited to, as it were, follow his gun."[10]

From *Wolfenstein 3D* onward, the kinds of avatars that players can adopt in FPS games have been relatively narrow. As Michael Hitchens has shown in a survey of FPS games, "military and related backgrounds continue to be the almost exclusive providers of FPS avatars, although this is perhaps understandable given the nature of such games."[11] It makes sense logically, as there is a narrative need for a character familiar with handling weapons; however, many FPS games are remarkably light on other narrative aspects to support the actions and choices made. In most cases, the player is a spy, soldier, or mercenary.

The influential Nintendo 64 game *GoldenEye 007*, based on the James Bond film *GoldenEye*, was released in 1997. Featuring a mission-based single-player mode, the critically acclaimed game took on the tropes of Ian Fleming's imperialist anti-Russian spy thrillers. In addition, it also introduced the multiplayer "death-match" mode, perhaps the most popular part of the game, which allowed multiple players to sit around the same console and play. This addition of multiplayer would later go on to become a key feature in the FPS genre. Despite the critique that could be made of the politics of Fleming's narrative as depicted in the game, the more popular mode was not the single-player, story-focused mode but the multiplayer one. This is the mode that most people played—myself included. The Nintendo 64 introduced social videogame play to a mass audience, with four-person competitions in front of many televisions. Playing *GoldenEye* was a social experience; the storylines mattered little, as did the characters —unless someone chose to play as "Oddjob," a character that was significantly shorter and therefore harder to hit.

Two years after *GoldenEye*'s release, PlayStation unveiled a key iteration in FPS: *Medal of Honor*. It allowed players to take on the fictional role of Jimmy Patterson, first a pilot and later an American spy, carrying out missions toward the end of the Second World War in Europe. The game's development was initiated by the filmmaker Steven Spielberg, who outlined the idea while in postproduction for *Saving Private Ryan*. The parallels between the two can be clearly seen in the game, particularly with both featuring scenes focusing on the D-Day landings on Omaha Beach in Normandy. To create his vision of the game, Spielberg employed Dale Dye, a former US Marine officer who had become a military advisor to Hollywood. Of the game that emerged, a reviewer wrote, "Not just a shoot 'em up, it offers miniature history lessons while you play, offering background on everything from the OSS to the Gestapo to V2 rockets while nostalgic art and video clips convey a sense of the period." As such, the "original Medal of Honor remains arguably the most educational FPS ever made."[12] However, in a sign of the future controversies over videogame violence, following the Columbine massacre the game also went through last-minute changes, in which all blood and gore was removed.[13]

Continuing the Second World War theme, the *Battlefield* series started with *Battlefield 1942* in 2002. It took the FPS genre in a more team-focused direction, providing larger multiplayer battles in which two teams fight over control points. This encouraged players on a team to coordinate and work together, trying to hold more control points than the other team, and in doing so competing to reduce the number of "tickets" of the opposing team to zero. The *1942* iteration featured historical background from that year, including weapons, vehicles, and a balanced competition between the Allies and the Axis. Others games in the series have focused on more contemporary events, while a 2016 installment, *Battlefield 1*, takes the First World War as its theme. The single-player aspect of the game focused on telling multiple stories. Explaining their approach, the developers said that they "wanted the player to see and feel what the characters are going through, rather than just experiencing it from behind their eyes."[14] However, as Julie Muncy warned before the release, it may perhaps not be the best idea to choose a setting that "many see as the epitome of wanton cruelty, a brutal and pointless stalemate that killed some 16 million people."[15] Those who grew up reading Wilfred Owen's poems would remember he warned against telling such stories to "children ardent for some desperate glory."[16] This is the first major instance that this historical moment has been mined for videogames. Before this, "aspects of WWI memory" have been "excluded at least partially because of their potentially controversial nature and the potential problems that games are perceived to face in engaging these issues."[17]

In a similar vein to these games, the incredibly successful *Call of Duty* series was launched in 2003. The first three installments covered the Second World War setting (as did the subsequent *World at War*) and involved the development team undertaking "extensive research to re-create everything as accurately as possible, including recording the sounds of the actual weapons firing, reloading, and so on."[18] As Owen Good, a videogames journalist, remarked, this brutal realism in the service of entertainment disrespects the memories of the individuals who actually experienced the war. On moving in with his grandfather, a marine colonel, Good decided "there was no way in hell he would ever see me playing that in his home," as he "was, literally, in a World War II first-person shooter in his youth—in one of the bloodiest battles of the Pacific campaign. And it wasn't entertainment."[19]

In this historical context, we often do not consider what the experience would be like to relive these events. Yet most players of these games are not reliving the experiences, but remembering specific things through play. Broadly speaking, there are two kinds of remembering taking place with FPS games. The first is what Marianne Hirsch has termed "postmemory," which denotes the relationship to historical events that happened before a person's birth.[20] This refracted kind of memory is how many of us now remember World War I and World War II—shaped as they are by film and other popular narrative accounts. As Adam Chapman argues, "Many historical videogames are amongst the most successful contemporary popular historical products."[21] This is particularly important given "the unpopularity of school history" and that "young people choose to use their free time playing videogames set in the past."[22] These kinds of games are not setting out to provide a nuanced historical account, but are focused instead on entertainment that draws on an attempt at realism. The focus on the player's actions makes the experience about them, rather than taking in the sociological sweep of devastation that a world war brings.

The second form of remembering is one in which we can still have a close connection to the events. An FPS game that serves as a good example is *Call of Duty 4: Modern Warfare*, which uses a more contemporary setting and a much more familiar frame of reference for the current generation. For many of the younger players in 2007, the Gulf War in 1990 and the invasion of Iraq in 2003 have become historical events. Again, the developers spent time at live-fire facilities, discussed the experiences with marines who had recently fought, and used veterans for motion capture and the design of artificial intelligence.[23] The game features a mission called "Death From Above," in which the player takes control of the gun turrets of an AC-130 gunship. The player directs the weaponry via "grainy, low-fi, 'white' or 'black hot' night vision," evoking the "real-life footage we've all seen, of laser-guided bombs and rattling chainguns destroying targets."[24] There is no direct risk to the player in this section, and it is a "scene as grimly and dispassionately realistic as any late night news report."[25]

The sequel, *Call of Duty: Modern Warfare 2*, follows similar themes, although the shock value is particularly ramped up in a level of the game titled "No Russian." Before the mission starts, there is an onscreen warning that what follows will feature disturbing material, and the player is offered the opportunity to skip the mission—something that only serves to further increase the shock value. The player, an undercover CIA agent, can participate in a mass shooting at an airport as a way to gain the trust of Russian terrorists. At no point is the player made to shoot into the crowds of civilians—although they can choose to participate actively rather than passively— but the Russian terrorists, whom the player cannot operate, will do so either way.

The successors to the *Modern Warfare* games, the *Call of Duty: Black Ops* series, turn to the Cold War era and focus on so-called black operations. This was a period of proxy wars, "fought with perfect moral clarity by people who funded them but didn't pick up a gun." It is this ethos that, Owen Good argues, *Call of Duty* "embodies," with its "repulsive vicariousness; its multiplayer-intensive focus, the kill-die-respawn-kill-die liturgy of the game's main selling point," without "even a metaphorical consequence for death in the game's principal mode of play."[26] The promotion of *Black Ops 2* even involved hiring Lieutenant Colonel Oliver North as a spokesman and consultant. North was a key actor in the Iran-Contra scandal in the 1980s (which is featured in the game), arranging the sale of US weapons to Iran while diverting money to fund the right-wing Contra rebels in Nicaragua; both of these activities were against US law. As Mark Lamia, head of development for the game, argued: "We're not trying to make a political statement with our game. We're trying to make a piece of art and entertainment.... For us to have met with him as we're creating our fiction is totally appropriate."[27]

This mixing of historical material with fiction makes a political statement whether or not the developers intend it as so. Using a figure like Oliver North normalizes the use of black operations and takes a position on a disturbing period of US history. This involves a desensitization to violence and militarism, building upon links between the military-industrial complex and the videogames industry. The importance of this form of memory is emphasized by Matthew Payne, who evokes Benedict Anderson's work on nationalism and "imagined communities."[28] The Gulf War, like many other imperialist conflicts, *did* happen. The stories that are then told about these events—both in the run-up to them and in their wake—shape the project of nationalism. A whole plethora of cultural artifacts form the "building blocks for our collective national memory, unifying disparate cultural groups across vast distances and eras," and Payne argues that videogames are becoming a key part of this process.[29]

Beyond remembering specific conflicts, whether through memory or postmemory, FPS games have further influence. This is also true of games more broadly, whether they extrapolate to different contexts in sci-fi (with the game *Halo* being a great example) or take other forms. As Payne reminds us, "A game does not have to explicitly reproduce our world to comment on it."[30] Yet, as we saw earlier, the links to the military-industrial complex highlight how games can actually exert an influence on our world. However, it is also entirely possible to play these videogames without accepting (critically or uncritically) the politics of the settings. The appeal of FPS games also lies in the feedback loops and the facilitation of flow within the game environment—the player's focus is often on the game mechanics and immediate decisions being made. There is no clear transmission mechanism through which the values of the game pass to the player. For example, in *GoldenEye* the flow players experience from the multiplayer competition is far removed from the politics of the game's single-player mode.

Nonetheless, when games address historical events or overlap with real-world politics, it is important to unpack what kinds of stories they are telling about the world. Another example worth examining is the long-running Tom Clancy–branded series of games. These are based on the technically specific, and arguably fetishistic, espionage and military books that Clancy authored. In particular, the *Splinter Cell* franchise focuses on Sam Fisher, an agent who operates beyond international law and rules of engagement. A 2013 installment, *Blacklist,* involves Fisher pitted against a terrorist group demanding the US recall all of its troops from abroad—a retreat that within the game is considered unimaginable. Fisher fights to ensure the US can continue to occupy other countries and threaten war against them. In a demo for the game shown at a gaming convention, there was a sequence in which Fisher enters a tent and kills two people and captures a third. Fisher questions the captive, and upon not receiving the answer he wants, proceeds to stab a knife into the captive's collarbone. At this point, the player can then control the motion of the knife with their controller until the graphically depicted man provides the answer. Although other graphic scenes were featured in *Splinter Cell's* predecessor, *Conviction*, this particular scene was later removed in favor of noninteractive "enhanced interrogation" (to use the American euphemism), offering only a "moral choice" after the terrorists' capture in which the player can "choose whether to kill or knock out his freshly tortured victim."[31]

This callous approach is reminiscent of the character Jack Bauer's in the TV series *24*, with the ends always justifying the means when dealing with terrorism. The popularization of this narrative can have a twofold effect: it normalizes torture as a necessary tool, and it advances the idea that the kind of intelligence generated by it can actually be useable. However, promoting the narrative simultaneously draws attention to these abhorrent practices. The moment described above in *Blacklist* is also a brief one that stands in stark contrast to the rest of the videogame, which mainly revolves around tense stealth action (not from an FPS perspective) and demands exacting skill from the player as they navigate around the map, dodging detection.

Half-Life, released in 1998, is not a war game in the sense of those I've just discussed, nor does it deal with torture. It is a sci-fi FPS featuring the theoretical physicist Gordon Freeman (although his voice is never heard, nor is he ever seen) and the opening of an interdimensional portal at the Black Mesa research facility. The entire game is experienced from the first-person viewpoint with no cutscenes, something that was quite unusual at the time it was released. It starts with the combat rookie Freeman, armed at first only with a crowbar, taking on both aliens and then the military. This game is important for both its legacy to the FPS genre and as the base game that was modded into *Counter-Strike*.

The current iteration, *Counter-Strike: Global Offensive* (or *CS:GO*), has updated the formula: in a two-sided team game, nondescript terrorists (Ts) face off against the counter-terrorists (CTs). In *CS:GO*'s most popular game mode, the competition boils down to one side planting a bomb while the other tries to defuse it. One side gets the terrorist's iconic weapon, the AK-47 rifle; the other side gets the US-made M4 assault rifle. *CS:GO* is an abstraction of terrorism into an equal-sided, time-limited, and repeatable competition. The short rounds of the game have no consequence beyond players adding to the overall score; any overt politics are replaced with the feedback loop of highly skilled competition against the other team. Yet familiar tropes appear here: the fact that the combatants are only men, the use of Middle Eastern and other stereotypical locales, and the Palestinian kaffiyehs the terrorists wear. There is no explanation for the terrorists' actions, leaving them only as the violent negation of the counter-terrorists—and presumably the West. However, rarely have I thought about the different settings and character models while playing *CS:GO*, a videogame I have regularly returned to over many years. It boils down the dynamics of the FPS genre to its most pure form and the appeal of its basic features: the combination of required skills and feedback loops.

A particular standout that differs from those above is the subversive *Spec Ops: The Line*. This was another iteration in a series, yet it was a significant and unexpected departure. As Kristine Jørgensen argues, it is a familiar game that uses the conventions of the FPS "but also somewhat subverts them."[32] The game starts with the familiar scene of the player riding in a helicopter, but it then crashes and the player is killed. From this unusual beginning, it goes back in time, and "things get worse from then on." The game riffs on *Apocalypse Now* in that a protagonist (Captain Martin Walker) serves as an unreliable narrator. I played this game without knowing the politics behind it, and the experience was unsettling. If you have not played it and think that you might, it would be worth it to try it yourself before reading this section.

At the start of *Spec Ops*, the mission is reconnaissance only; however, this rapidly accelerates into more and more killing. For example, at one point Walker and his two allies attack an enemy base. They assassinate a lookout and spot what looks like "an army," then notice an unattended mortar. When Walker orders it to be set up, one ally exclaims, "You're fucking kidding right? That's white phosphorous . . . you've seen what that shit does? You know we can't—"

He is interrupted by the other: "We might not have a choice."

"There's always a choice," the first ally replies.

The protagonist answers, "No, there's really not," and proceeds to take control of the mortar.

Through the same grainy-camera view featured in the "Death from Above" scene in *Call of Duty*, the bombs are directed from above, albeit this time a reflection of Walker's emotionless face is just visible. Unlike in *Call of Duty*, the next part of the scene involves entering the area directly after the carnage. The team moves through and encounters a fatally wounded soldier who simply asks, "Why? . . ." and then says, "We were helping them." It then moves to a cutscene that shows the team walking over the bodies of hundreds of civilians burned alive during the onslaught. This moment marks where the storyline descends into a "dark narrative of post-traumatic stress syndrome and a military operation gone horribly wrong." However, what makes this moment different from one commonly depicted in film is "the sense of being involved in the events—not only by witnessing them, but through the sense of being *complicit* to the actions that take place in the game."[33]

Spec Ops is an imagined conflict, not one based on historical events. The narration from Walker gets increasingly unreliable as the game progresses, "down into the abyss of war crimes and eventually to a point where death may seem like the better end-game option."[34] As Daniel Joseph has argued, the game is "an abomination, a demon child retched up from the video game industry."[35] This was not the first attempt to revive the *Spec Ops* series, yet the developer YAGER took on the challenge, despite not having experience in this area. In what was later described as a fraught relationship between the developer and publisher, something quite different to the "military-game jingoism and fun core loops of killing and shooting" was created.[36] The resulting game poses rhetorical questions like, "What kind of person likes virtual killing enough to spend hours engaged in it?" It uses the interactive format to provide a reflexive experience, quite unlike other FPS games. It is fun (in a sense), in that it still draws on the FPS perspective and draws the player in, but it also provides a space to think about how and why these games are appealing. *Spec Ops* is a game I continue to think about from time to time, an experience that has left a mark on my understanding of video-games. It also points toward other ways of making and playing games about military violence.

What can be gleaned from FPS games is that they have a close relationship with the military—either directly or indirectly—along with an often-explicit set of ideological positions about war. These games are experienced through the first-person perspective, allowing players to "see" war, not only through virtual eyes, but also mostly from the perspective of American imperialism. Although players may code and decode these experiences in different ways, they are all asked in some way to reflect and act upon the ideology of military conflict and imperialism. The FPS game also goes further than other military games: it positions the player as a key actor, decisive in shifting events. This is clearly not the case in war—a single soldier did not win historical battles, nor are contemporary conflicts the product of one person. That position of the player also makes these games a powerfully escapist experience, and one that is not so straightforward as in games where players choose how to play these games.

ROLE-PLAYING, SIMULATIONS, AND STRATEGY

██ hile analyzing FPS videogames is important for making sense of play, there are also many other genres and formats that can expand our understanding. Of particular interest here are role-playing, simulation, and strategy games.

Role-playing games (RPGs) clearly involve the aspects of simulation (or what Caillois called *mimicry*),[1] allowing the player to step into another character and thinking how that character would act in a given scenario. Many videogames draw on the traditions of pen-and-paper role-playing games like *Dungeons & Dragons*, involving character creation, but with the videogame handling the functions of "dungeon master" and the rolling of dice. This significantly lowers the barriers for role-playing, no longer requiring the physical presence, coordination, and detailed expertise of players. *Baldur's Gate* and *The Elder Scrolls* series are prime examples of the scale and scope of these kinds of RPGs, with their high-fantasy setting and open-ended and free-form gameplay. These kinds of videogames yield two kinds of experiences. The first is escapism. The games often involve power fantasies in which the player character grows in strength and challenges some kind of great threat or evil. The second is storytelling. Similar to FPS games (whether the RPG is experienced first person or through some other viewpoint), the RPG form allows the player to experience a story as an active participant.

The stories that are told through RPGs differ on the basis of the player's choices. For example, in *Deus Ex*, which allows the player to explore and interact with a bleak cyberpunk world, the scenarios can be completed in multiple ways, with both violent and nonviolent options. Each playthrough offers different storylines in which the player can experiment with their own agency and how it affects a global conspiracy. Here it is worth comparing this medium to film. While the *Star Wars* films offer a clear-cut "good" versus "evil" perspective, the game *Star Wars: Knights of the Old Republic II* offers a far more nuanced take because the player is able to explore these themes through their own choices. In *Arcanum: Of Steamworks and Magick Obscura*, the themes of high fantasy are explored within the tumult of an industrial revolution, whereas the retro-futuristic *Fallout* series deals with large themes like the pointlessness of war and nuclear apocalypse. These examples, along with many others, not only provide backdrops upon which storytelling takes place; their format also creates a space within which players can read events and tell stories from very different perspectives, as well as choose how they interact with the people they meet and the factions they encounter. These interactions can be informed and read in a multitude of ways.

The kinds of stories that these videogames tell are important, but so too are the ways in which the stories are constructed. These rule-bound systems always have their limits, and even RPGs with multiple-path options have their constraints. Part of the challenge is playing within worlds and pushing up against these constraints and experimenting with how far the player can go. Many RPG games begin with a player-creation option, giving the sense of a customizable experience. However, "depending on what's included or shown, we can glean the developer's stances about race and gender, amongst other things. Maybe they don't feel a race or gender is important enough to include, for example."[2] There are often far more options for Caucasian characters, with limitations on the portrayal of characters' voicing, accents, skin tone, hair types, and so on. These are not the kinds of game-based constraints that are fun to experiment with through play;

instead, these are imbued with biases that naturalize some elements within the gameplay, even before the game begins. Some aspects need to be challenged, particularly when a game claims to allow the player to shape the world through their actions. Critiquing these aspects is not about critiquing the entire game but rather to push for a game world in which a broader range of experiences and options can be explored.

Beyond the RPG games with a single-character focus are the larger simulation games. *Populous* is an early example in which the player takes on the role of a "god." The player is assigned a top-down view, able to interact from above, helping or hindering their followers. This abstraction in viewpoint from the first-person perspective is clearly a power fantasy, one allowing players to interact with models of the world. From this starting point marked by *Populous*, the top-down perspective evolves in broadly three directions. The first is that of *The Sims*, in which players take this perspective to play with what is essentially a "digital dollhouse." This is one of the most popular videogame series ever, selling over 200 million copies.[3] As Jon-Paul Dyson, director of the International Center for the History of Electronic Games, has argued: "The game has had universal appeal, with female players outnumbering males, and adults as passionate about the game as children.... And by turning the computer into a toy to explore the complexity of the human experience, *The Sims* radically expanded the notion of what a game could be."[4] While this is an important point, it is also worth thinking about the kinds of stories that are possible to tell within the game. It presents the player with what is essentially a digital sandbox—there are no defined goals. Instead, the player looks after the needs and moods of the virtual inhabitants. However, there are limitations on how these can be addressed, mainly involving the formation of a functional household in which the adults work and purchase various commodities in a reinforcing cycle. The designer, Will Wright, has explained that originally *The Sims* was intended as a satire of consumer culture; however, this seems to have gotten lost along the way.[5] Nonetheless, players find ways to tell other stories or toy with the "sims." In one infamous example, players realized they could essentially kill a sim by removing the ladder to their pool, leaving the sim unable to climb out and causing them to eventually drown. As a developer on *The Sims 4* noted, "[The] player reaction to a Sims game without pools was so intense that developers knew they had to rectify the situation as soon as possible."[6]

The *SimCity* series exists on a larger scale. The subject is the city rather than the household, drawing the focus onto a larger and more anonymous mass of citizens. *SimCity* taps into a similar sandbox/dollhouse experience. It also often demonstrates how much more effectively the player could handle traffic problems than local government in the real world. The city begins as a tabula rasa, with the player able to generate the landscape from which they can begin planning the city. In various iterations this involves ever more ways to lay out the city—from the basic zoning on a grid-based pattern to the more complex organization of utilities, transport, and public services. While this kind of power fantasy provides a way for a player to imagine they could centrally plan an entire city, it develops in a linear direction, mainly involving problems emerging as the city grows that can then be solved with a new technology or technique.

Unfortunately, this is far removed from the reality of contemporary cities and their construction histories, which rest upon centuries of planning restrictions and dispersed decision making. It also leaves out the way in which cities are shaped too by the resistance and organizing of the people who live there. Those who are spied from above in the game might complain about bad traffic or petition for a new amenity, but the decision to respond to those concerns is left with the player. This fails to address the reality of a city like London (where I live) and how it is marked by class struggle—both from above and from below.

However, it is a little unfair to critique a simulation for not including everything. After all, a simulation is an abstraction, and requires each dynamic in the simulation to be coded. It would be quite a challenge to code an accurate representation of resistance and gentrification into a city since people's struggles are much harder to abstract from than traffic or weather models. The problem is, "to code something, to include something at all in a game is to define how it works."[7] Because the process of coding a videogame involves deciding what is and isn't included, it is therefore a political act in both obvious and subtle ways. Despite these limitations, these kinds of sandboxes also allow for utopian experimentation, as is evident in the endgame of *Sim-City*, in which the player can construct massive arcologies, not only pointing to an alternative way of organizing the city, but eventually, in the case of a recent release in the *Civilization* series, leaving Earth and colonizing space.

Operating on a wider scale, the *Civilization* series of games allows the player to guide an entire society from 4000 BCE to the future. I want to focus particularly on *Civilization*, among thousands of possible titles, for two reasons: one, the game deals specifically with history at a societal level, making it a particularly good candidate for exploring with Marx and his method of historical materialism; and two, *Civilization* remains one of my favorites, a series that has been running for almost all of my life.

The game was first released in 1991, an influential example of the "4X" videogame, a term referring to the four routes in which a player can achieve victory: "eXplore," "eXpand," "eXploit," and "eXterminate." The turn-based game allows the player to make choices about the organization and direction of a civilization. As the series' creator, Sid Meier, has explained, "I prefer games where the player can lead the game in the direction that they want ... and then they kind of end up with that unique story that only they can know."[8] The games facilitated the rise of emergent storytelling, an incredibly compelling videogame feature. The shape of the landscape you start with in the game, the progress of your different cities and their relative success, the interactions with friendly and unfriendly civilizations you encounter—all of these lead to different stories the player can read onto the game, "experimenting" along the way (to add another "X" into the mix).

Again, in these virtual sandboxes, the player is free to choose the things they want to do. However, the 4X game often omits important parts of human history. For example, there are no slaves in *Civilization*, "and some have criticized the game for that glaring historical omission."[9] In an interview, Meier offered an explanation for why his team left out contentious features of human history like slavery:

> One of the things we really try to avoid in our games is this kind of—"this choice would be the right thing to do, but this choice is gonna help me win the game"—put the players in those kind of moral dilemmas. That's not what our games are about. We want you to feel good about yourself when you finish the game.[10]

Given that slavery played such a key role in the formation of industrial capitalism, this is not missing one moment of history, but erasing a core part of it.[11]

What *Civilization* does is provide the player with a set of rules to accompany their sandbox. Meier explains: "You are dealing with clear, intuitive rules, and basing your strategy on them interacting. . . . How they interact with each other, and how you make the tradeoffs, is where the interest lies, where the interesting decisions show up."[12] However, the game implies that these rules are neutral, in spite of the omission of slavery and other "moral dilemmas" (as Meier refers to them). History is conceived as a linear progression for thousands of years, with new technologies incrementally and gradually improving society.

Meier has explained that he and his team "embrace the progress theory of civilizations" but that he "know[s] that can be controversial."[13] They considered implementing a "rise and fall" dynamic in the game, but found that "people are not inclined to enjoy the 'fall' part" and stopped playing. Despite the limitations of the model of history used in *Civilization*, Meier believed in the game and what it can reveal:

> It reflects some fundamental truths about civilization, but it is not intended to be the final word on how civilizations work.

I think it does a good job of showing how small turning points—you know, the butterfly effect—that small changes can take history off in completely different directions. We tend to take for granted that history kind of had to work out the way it did. But one of the lessons of *Civilization*, which I think is true, is that with a few little changes, things could have gone differently.[14]

The game therefore still provides a compelling, if partial, sandbox in which some of these dynamics can be explored. Again, as I mentioned earlier, this critique is not to say that the game is unplayable—the reality is that these kinds of games are incredibly compelling. However, pointing to these limits with the rules of the sandbox is also an important part of thinking through history, perhaps pointing toward what other kinds of simulations one could seek to achieve. The problem is that it is very difficult to take history—what Colin Campbell calls "the chaos of human events"—and "render it into highly predictable systems that always do what the player expects them to do."[15] But this is exactly what these kinds of videogames do, trying to present "the development of history with a clear chain of cause and effect."[16] Typically, these predictable systems are organized in the three key areas of economics, politics, and war (later versions of *Civilization* also include culture), and the player progresses through the game by gaining points that they then use to dominate their opponents. This naturalizes capitalism, with its dynamics of accumulation, imperialism, and conflict. While the game allows experimentation with different choices over the course of human history, these choices are limited by the rules—similar to how different possibilities of making games are narrowed by the use of software development kits, as I discussed in part 1.

Alternative systems of governance are available in *Civilization*, but they have a limited effect on the gameplay. For example, the Communist movement is reduced to three gameplay modifiers in *Civilization VI*, for example: "land units gain +4 Defense Strength," "+0.6 Production per Citizen in cities with Governors," and "+15% Production in all cities." Instead of a future classless society of emancipated workers, it is boiled down to stronger units and additional production, equivalent to the militarization and five-year plans of Stalinist Russia. This is what Hal Draper refers to as "socialism from above," a socialism "*handed down* to the grateful masses in one form or another, by a ruling elite which is not subject to their control." This is not the kind of process that we would argue for based on the Marxism applied in this book. Draper contrasts "socialism from above" with "socialism from below," which can "be realized only through the self-emancipation of activized masses in motion, reaching out for freedom with their own hands, mobilized 'from below' in a struggle to take charge of their own destiny, as actors (not merely subjects) on the stage of history."[17] However, introducing this kind of system within *Civilization* would be very hard to do, as it would mean the player relinquishing control to their empowered virtual masses. No doubt the right thing to do, but less fun for the player as they would no longer be needed!

These kinds of points are important given that there was also an educational iteration of the game, called *CivilizationEDU*, that was designed to be used in schools. It was proposed to "provide students with the opportunity to think critically and create historical events, consider and evaluate the geographical ramifications of their economic and technological decisions, and engage in systems thinking and experiment with the causal/correlative relationships between military, technology, political and socioeconomic development."[18] While *Civilization* can definitely provide some insights into historical geopolitics, we also need to think about how, as Marx and Engels argued, "the ideas of the ruling class are in every epoch the ruling ideas, i.e., the class which is the ruling material force of society, is at the same time its ruling intellectual force."[19] This means that radical ideas or different interpretations of events may be blocked, either because of their direct competition with the dominant ideas, or, in the case of *Civilization*, the game's rules block other ways of acting or exploring history. While *CivilizationEDU* was an attempt to make the game more accurate for educational purposes, it still prevented the exploration of alternative ways of running society, thus reinforcing a capitalist worldview.

The linear progression of *Civilization* is a long way from the historical materialist approach introduced by Marx. *Civilization* is obviously missing a nuanced understanding of class struggle as the basis for understanding history, but this also should come as no surprise. The mechanics of simulations or strategy games place agency with a player who is directing from above, whereas Marxism follows a ground-level perspective ("socialism from below") based on the mass self-activity of the working class. Therefore, in *Civilization*, Marxist dynamics are reduced to a minimum or excluded entirely from the game's set of rules, or they are replaced instead with a Stalinist perspective ("socialism from above"). However, it should be remembered that *Civilization* is not an attempt to model society in all its complexities, and despite its problems, it presents a sandbox in which history can—within limits—be explored.

Alpha Centauri, one of the later iterations of *Civilization*, presents the player with quite-different choices. The game starts where the previous installments usually end, with the launching of a spaceship to the nearest habitable planet. The player can experiment with seven ideologically different factions (expanded later to fourteen), each with a vision for how to remake society in this new world. The alien world is itself a faction of sorts, with which the player can either fight or find new ways to enjoy coexistence. This kind of sandbox allows for a reflection on contemporary ideologies, expressed in a different context, albeit still from a top-down perspective—both visually and politically. In either case, the *Civilization* series are still very playable videogames, so addictive that today's gaming custom of "just one more turn" traces back to the original game in the series.[20]

POLITICAL VIDEOGAMES

To critique these genres of videogames, as I've done in the previous chapters, is not to say that these videogames should not be played, just as we can critique Hollywood and still critically enjoy watching the films it releases. However, as the Hollywood movie is not the only kind of film, so are there a variety of games in the videogame industry worth our analysis. Among them is an expanding genre of "political videogames."

When I was a postdoctoral researcher, I worked on a short-lived project about videogames that shed light on the political significance not only of the political game genre but of videogames in general. The project was funded to explore the impact and potential of videogames, both in regard to their development and their play. During this time, I saw the potential—both good and bad—of videogames. The project manager imported techniques from the tech and videogames industry, including Monday-morning "huddle"-style meetings, KPIs (key performance indicators), and something called "sunset goals." To decide the direction of the project, we "played" a tarot-style board game to pick archetypes for the general character of the project, like "the trickster," "the child," and so on. These were inspired by Carl Jung but had little, if anything, to do with conducting an academic research project. The initial notion was that adopting the managerial practices from the tech and videogames industry would suddenly result in accelerated academic outputs—it may be no surprise to hear that it did not. "Gamification" was a term we regularly used, referring to the application of game-like aspects to other contexts. We approached it as a concept that could be applied in countless settings, improving education, fitness, health, productivity, and so on. This was what many on the project set out to do. It was impressive how much we believed that games could have an impact on the world.

What was missing from the project's focus was the effect that gamification was already having in the real world. When I worked in a call center as part of an inquiry for my last book, I saw firsthand the use of gamification at work. The call center was filled with ways to collect metrics and measure worker performance. At the simplest level, the large screen over the call center floor compared each worker's performance in real time by ranking them from best seller to worst. While this never convinced me to try my hardest to reach the top of the leader board, it certainly motivated me to try a little harder so as not to stay in last place for the entire shift. After all, poor performance could result in my sacking with little or no notice. And there were more sophisticated forms of gamification the managers deployed to try and motivate workers. For example, workers were asked to play games before a shift to as a way to coax workers into a mood conducive to performing emotional labor on the phones. Other kinds of competitions would be organized, either between individual workers or teams, with prizes or penalties as incentives. In what would later turn out to be a revealing finding, the most powerful incentive to make a sale was the reward of being able to leave early. No other prize—claiming the top spot on the leader board, winning shopping vouchers, or anything else—could motivate people as much as not having to stay in that gamified workplace.[1]

Within the other research project I worked on, there was no recognition at all of the extensive reach of gamification. Instead, games were seen only as some sort of panacea for the drudgery and boredom of the modern world, shorn from the economic and social realities that most of the world faces each day. Despite people's refusal to engage with the question of power, gamification is political. For example, one of the team's research suggestions (raised after I had left the project, I am keen to point out) was collaborating with the police to make a videogame that simulated different strategies to control protests. Team members presented this as a neutral tool that would aid both the police and demonstrators. However, there was no recognition of the role that the police have played in demonstrations, from injuring and killing protestors to actively seeking to quash dissent. Similarly, there was no suggestion that protestors could have access to the game to plan their own strategies. One can only imagine what kinds of brutal strategies a police commander would try to test out in a videogame. What is certain is it would have been a very *political* game.

While my former collaborators did not see their project in these terms, the recent growth of explicitly political videogames as a genre suggests why this perspective is justified. I turn to this genre now with the aim to discuss how politics and activism can be expressed in videogames—both by looking at "political" videogames, and by considering the ways that *all* videogames are political in varying ways.

Among the recent wave of political videogames are a notable number of titles inspired by or linked with left-wing politics. These kinds of games are explicitly political. But it is worth noting that, to quote Patricia Hernandez, "when the real world seeps into games," some people "don't like it, because it ruins the whole 'escapism' thing." However, she continues, "there's no such thing as an apolitical game and thinking otherwise can be dangerous."[2] All videogames are political. As Mike Cook has stated, political videogames have potential to change player's ideas, but "we have to make sure that we're aware of the power of persuasion, misdirection and bias, and keep a critical but open mind."[3]

Before turning to discuss political videogames, it is first worth considering the long history of political games. Beginning in the early 1970s, Bertell Ollman, a Marxist professor from New York, set about thinking through what a left-wing political board game would involve. On playing *Monopoly*, he noticed that the game does something unusual. People "play Monopoly as individuals and take individual credit or blame for the result. Skill and luck are each considered personal qualities. In neither case can anyone else be blamed if you lose."[4] Yet this bears little relation to the actual experience of property accumulation under capitalism: "There is a real monopoly game going on, but you haven't been invited to play. More than likely, you could not afford the stakes." Ollman then set out to find "the critical, and especially the socialist, game." In the process, he discovered that in the over four thousand years of board game history, there have been examples of what might be considered political games. Ollman asks: "Is it only a coincidence that in chess, the medieval game *par excellence*, a knight or a bishop can corner a king?" He also gives the example of *Roarem Castle*, a game dating back to nineteenth-century England that "satirizes the lives of the still-powerful aristocracy."[5]

Through this research, Ollman stumbled upon a version of *Monopoly* called *Anti-Monopoly*. It turned out not to be what he was looking for, but he did learn something meaningful from the game's creator, Ralph Anspach: *Monopoly* had actually been intended "as a critique of the very system it has done so much to promote."[6] Anspach claimed that the real inventor of *Monopoly* was a Quaker named Elizabeth Magie. The game was invented in 1903 and originally called *The Landlord's Game*, featuring tiles named "Lord Blueblood's Estate" and "The Soakum Lighting Co." By 1925 the game became known as *Monopoly* and featured the following text in the introduction:

> Monopoly is designed to show the evil resulting from the institution of private property. At the start of the game, every player is provided with the same chance of success as every other player. The game ends with one person in possession of all the money. What accounts for the failure of the rest, and what one factor can be singled out to explain the obviously ill-adjusted distribution of the community's wealth, which this situation represents? Those who win will answer "skill." Those who lose will answer "luck." But maybe there will be some, and these, while admitting the element of skill and luck, will answer with Scott Nearing [a socialist writer of the time] "private property."[7]

This is a pretty clear anti-capitalist message for the game. However, the modern version changed that introductory text to read, "The idea of the game is to buy and rent or sell property so profitably that one becomes the wealthiest player and eventually monopolist."[8] The game's mechanics—"the lopsided accumulation of wealth"—draw on two of Caillois's notions—*agôn* (competition) and *alea* (chance)—in the process transforming what is the systemic problem of capitalism into something that is celebrated.[9] However, unlike in the real world, each player begins with the same amount of wealth. This is because for the game to be fun, Ollman argues, the players have to have an equal starting point.

Ollman then struggled with this problem of how to design a game that could focus on inequality, but that people would want to play. His solution was the board game *Class Struggle*. While it is not that easy to track down today, the Interference Archive in New York has a copy, which I have seen but unfortunately not played. The game tries to overcome the problem posed by *Monopoly* by having players assume the roles of classes rather than those of individuals. The premise is that "capitalists and workers" are "roughly equal in power, though of course the sources of their power are very different."[10] The board game was made and distributed, with an image of Karl Marx arm wrestling Nelson Rockefeller on the box's cover. The chance cards have messages such as "You are treating your class allies very badly" and "Your son has become a follower of Reverend [Sun Myung] Moon." Scrawled on the middle of the board are the phrases "Socialism (The Workers Win!)" and Barbarism (The Capitalists Win!)." The game went on to sell 230,000 copies when it was launched in 1978. While the story of the process of distributing the game is interesting, it is worth drawing attention to the fact that "a small group of striking workers at Brentano's Bookstore asked him [Ollman] to pull the game." When he refused, they thought he was a sellout trying to make money off workers, and "then used his refusal to promote their own fight."[11] So the game itself became part of class struggle too. Despite this, Ollman maintained his faith in his project's potential, later noting: "As long as there is a class struggle ... there is a great need to help young people understand what it is, how it works, and where they fit into it.... The game could still contribute to this important work."[12]

This pedagogic, or teaching, element is particularly powerful with games as it allows players to interact and experiment with a system. In this way, videogames hold possibilities for doing what Ollman tried with board games. The political games made by Paolo Pedercini and published on the website Molleindustria are a good example. His *Phone Story* is pitched as "an educational game about the dark side of your favorite smart phone. Follow your phone's journey around the world and fight the market forces in a spiral of planned obsolescence."[13] Designed for smartphone devices, the game "attempts to provoke a critical reflection on its own technological platform." It is based around four mini-games, each covering a part of the supply chain, from coltan mining in the Congo, factory workers in China, e-waste in Pakistan, and consumerism in the Global North. The plan for the game was to redirect the proceeds (which was 70 percent after iTunes took its 30 percent cut) to grassroots organizations that are fighting corporate abuses.

Phone Story was banned from iTunes three hours after launch. Apple claimed that it breached rules on charity donations as well as two guidelines regarding "depictions of 'violence or abuse of children,' and 'excessively objectionable or crude content.'" However, as noted by a journalist at the time, "the former appears to be crucial to the satirical intent of the game, while the latter is something of a grey area—who is most likely to object to the content here: users or Apple?"[14] The game remained available on Android, and through revenue across the various platforms raised $6,000. This total was much less than expected (though it did earn an impressive $630 on iTunes in the three short hours it was available). The *Phone Story* team decided that the money raised "won't do that much to an organization but [it] could be significant for an individual who used to earn about $130 a month." The money was donated to Tian Yu, a worker who suffered serious injuries after trying to commit suicide while working at Foxconn.[15]

There are three aspects of this videogame that are worth exploring. The first is that it uses the hardware as part of the intervention. The mini-games explore the supply chains that the hardware relies upon. These supply chains are often hidden from the end user, so the act of making these visible is political. The website for *Phone Story* also contains a number of pages explaining the processes and providing further reading. For example, the discussion of "obsolescence" begins with the following:

> When you purchased this phone, it was new and sexy. You've been waiting for it for months. No evidence of its troubling past was visible. Did you really need it? Of course you did. A lot of money was invested to instill this desire in you. You were looking for something that could signal your status, your dynamic lifestyle, your unique personality. Just like everyone else.

This is the second point. The videogame plays on the position of the player as the owner of a smartphone to reflect on the economic and social relations, not only of the supply chain external to them, but also of the player's own role in purchasing and consuming the product. The videogame can therefore be quite an unsettling experience, with the potential to leave the player with a different understanding of a device they use daily. As stated in Molleindustria's mission statement, the aim is to "reappropriate video games as a popular form of mass communication" and "investigate the persuasive potentials of the medium by subverting mainstream video gaming cliché."[16] The third point is that the videogame goes beyond just propaganda: it uses the money it raised for a political end. In the process, it also highlights the large cut of 30 percent that distribution platforms take—an excessive amount. Molleindustria may not have reached its goal of raising enough to fund organizations fighting in the resistance, but the money did benefit someone within the brutal phone supply chain.

There are a range of other games released by Molleindustria that take different experimental angles on politicizing videogames. *To*

Build a Better Mousetrap is a "management" videogame in which the player runs a "semi-abstract" mousetrap factory, employing and choosing how much to pay the mice-workers.[17] As one commentator noted, "[Pedercini's] done something very difficult, which is to clearly, concisely and with a shockingly dark sense of humor explain the way that our economic system is gamed against working people, by making players recreate it."[18] Molleindustria also released the part-videogame, part–digital art installation *May-Day NetParade*, developed in 2004 for the political day of action known as EuroMayDay. This was a "virtual demo" that players could join using their own avatar creations, but they had to do so before the date of the demonstration. This process both promoted the demonstration beforehand and left a lasting mark that could be traced afterward. Other games by the developer include *Unmanned*, which covers a day in the life of a drone pilot, and *A Short History of the Gaze*, "an experiential essay for Virtual Reality" that explores the relationship between the player's gaze (or viewpoint) and violence that is so common in games.

Another of Molleindustria's videogames that is worth discussing here is *Every day the same dream*. In this game, the player controls an office worker within a bleak world marked by a drab grayscale palette. The player is only offered a few options: they can move left or right and choose to interact with select objects. Within this simple control scheme, the player goes through the routine of an office worker, focusing on the banality of the tasks. As David Leblanc has noted, it "is an exercise in boredom, one that moves me to think at the same time, *this game is boring and I do not want to play it*, and, *I recognize this feeling of work and want catharsis*."[19] If the player sticks with it (and here I won't spoil the experience for those who have not tried it), there are some small moments of refusal that they can explore. These actions then shift the narrative for the next day, which otherwise would have been a repeat of the day before. Playing the videogame—if "playing" can be the right term here—allows the player to explore the themes of alienation, estrangement, and refusal. Leblanc quotes the German playwright Bertolt Brecht to make sense of this: "When the rules emerging from this life in society are treated as imperfect and provisional . . . the theatre leaves its spectators productively disposed even after the spectacle is over."[20] This is the potential of playing through *Every day the same dream*: to upset the notion of work, to question and even subvert the uncanny reality it displays as "normal."[21]

This use of videogame rules to convey the dynamics of a given system are also used in *Papers, Please*. In that game, the player takes on the role of an immigration officer in the imaginary Stalinist country of Arstotzka. As with *Every day the same dream*, the game mechanics here are repetitive and banal. The main choice the player makes is whether to approve or deny an individual's entry to the country. It is a videogame about bureaucracy, about examining paperwork to make choices that could drastically affect the lives of others. Game reviewer John Walker said the following about how the game explores bureaucracy:

> Its lofi graphics and static setting join its focus on mundanity and repetition under pressure to suggest something that sounds about as far away from "game" as you might imagine. And yet [it] remains an engrossing, creeping affair, almost rogue-like in its grip on you to last longer, work faster, abandon principles more freely, and compromise integrity with ever-more consummate ease.[22]

The process of choosing who to approve and deny is complicated by the fact that the player is paid per each person processed and faces the pressure of needing to make enough money to provide for a family. The spot-the-difference mechanics make the game play out like a puzzle game, while the narrative pushes the player forward. As Walker noted, *Papers, Please* "explores that intriguing space between what you'll do to see a narrative progress, and what you're just too uncomfortable to do even in fiction."[23] In the process it uses a rule-based system to allow players to explore how far they can push, along with depicting the consequences of bureaucracy.

This War of Mine takes on the common theme of military conflict. However, the game subverts it, by giving the player control of a group of civilians attempting to survive in a city in the middle of a modern military conflict. At night, the player can direct members of the party to head out to scavenge. This can be achieved by bartering or stealing, but the videogame also offers the option of fighting and killing. While this feature speaks to the desperation of trying to survive in a war zone, it nevertheless feels like *This War of Mine* is falling back into the mechanics of more traditional war games. Still, the sense of danger in the videogame feels different to other games in which the world is viewed through the barrel of a gun; one videogame journalist writes: "There is danger everywhere—from snipers to other civilians to the diseases that come when cities break down. The one thing you don't do is pick up a gun and fight back."[24]

In a way, these kinds of videogames are aimed at an already politically inclined audience. This is not to doubt that some players may have come across these and found them engaging on their own terms, but they are pitched as "political" games. As Marijam Didžgalvytė has noted, "There is an abundance of politically-motivated games, but are they ever going to change anyone's opinion from one side to another?"[25] She makes her point by drawing on a quote by the Swedish fine art curator Maria Lind: "If, when you are about to tell a joke, you make the declaration 'This is going to be really funny!,' then in all likelihood the listener is not going to find the joke funny."

Didžgalvytė points out as an important exception one videogame that has had a much bigger impact than others. *The Uber Game* was released through the website of *Financial Times*, which is not known for its left-wing views. The browser-based game starts by asking the player, "Can you make it in the gig economy?" Then the player is allowed to explore what it is like to work for Uber, making choices along the way. The game ends with the total earnings the player has managed to make, but then Uber's cut of the fares, along with all the expenses—the lease on the car, gas, insurance, any repairs, and so on—are taken off.

When the player sees how much they have actually made, they see "they've often been earning only half of the minimum wage." As Didžgalvytė explains, "The game's point is obvious and its effect is striking, not least because it's in a place to be played by the *Financial Times* readership—a group of people that generally praise the gig economy, and its lack of bothersome unionisation."[26] Again, here, the rules of the game provide a reflection of society's unequal rules. The mechanics work to highlight the lack of agency that Uber drivers have to make a living wage. Although I have now spoiled the outcome for any reader who has not yet played, the realization that comes at the end for the first-time player is one of genuine surprise that cannot be foreseen at the start of the game.

Besides these videogames about work, there are other examples of politically themed videogames. In the US there have been many variants of anti–Donald Trump games, like *Punch the Trump*. In the UK, a videogame called *Corbyn Run* was released to support the Labour Party, under the leadership of Jeremy Corbyn, in the 2017 election. The player takes on the role of a pixelated Jeremy Corbyn, running after the then prime minister Theresa May and another Conservative politician. There is a battle bus labeled "Lies," referencing the additional money that the Brexit campaign leaders promised for the National Health Service and failed to deliver, as well as the ghost of Margaret Thatcher. As Marijam Didžgalvytė notes, "It's a fairly linear form of entertainment as (admittedly amusing) propaganda."[27] There are no game mechanics to convey some feature of capitalism, nor a structural critique of society. As Rosa Carbo-Mascarell, one of the developers, explained: "It was important to us to seem accessible, while still maintaining a level of political satire. Since launching, we've received a number of messages from people saying they've changed their vote, thanks to the game."[28] Unlike *Class Struggle*, designed with the more ambitious aim of producing a tool for political education, *Corbyn Run* was intended to push a clear message in the run-up to an election through a contemporary medium. In this way, "*Corbyn Run* is another form of essential engagement, at a time when young, perhaps first-time voters are being courted by politicians and party supporters more vocally than ever before."[29]

So far in this discussion, we could say that there are two different kinds of political videogames: the explicitly "political," which are often marketed as such; and those, as identified by Didžgalvytė, designed to actually achieve a political outcome. The latter are an example of the old maxim "show, don't tell"; instead of declaring the intention beforehand, they allow people to make up their own minds. Didžgalvytė explains:

> Good art gives rise to new insights, while better art arms the spectator with tools for concrete action. Video gaming's immersive properties are unequalled by any other medium, and has the potential to teach and share tools that question the status quo, both implicitly and explicitly.[30]

The politics of videogames can also be revealed in their escapist allure, in that they tell us something about what people are escaping from. Raymond Tsang, an esports professional better known by his *League of Legends* handle "KaSing," serves as a good example. In a 2016 interview, KaSing outlines the appeal of professional esports. At the age of nineteen, he decided to dedicate himself full time to becoming a professional videogame player. His chosen game, *League of Legends*, as noted earlier, has an estimated one hundred million monthly players. KaSing, originally from Tottenham in North London, made the choice of career against his parents. As he explains:

> First of all, I wanted to go pro even while I was in college . . . because I didn't think I would want to live a normal life where I have a job nine to five and not enjoy it at all. . . . In a way, if you can go through this barrier, even if you're not getting any help or support, and if you have the fortitude or mentality to ignore it and just do what you want, then I think this is one of the most important things that you can have. You need a strong mind.[31]

He outlines how this offered a better alternative to working a typical job, echoing the refusal-of-work approach that sprang up at the birth of videogames. This is akin to a phenomenon my colleague Mark R. Johnson and I encountered in interviews with Twitch streamers: people who try to make a living from live streaming their own videogame play to online audiences. Their motivation is also tied up with a sense that anyone could do it, but that "in the end it's all about you and it's all about you working your hardest."[32]

Very few people have the opportunity of escaping the drudgery of work to play videogames as a professionalized job. In actuality, professional players face a reality of training schedules and competition pressure that in some ways alters their sense of videogames as play. The much more common experience is that videogame play aligns with the refusal-of-work approach. For example, Sid Meier used to design videogames with a "boss key," which allowed the player to "hit a special key, and a spreadsheet would pop up on the screen so you could pretend you were doing your job."[33] Similarly, "playing games on the job was seen by managers as the most corrosive habit of a computerized labor force."[34] Many office computers run software specifically designed to prevent workers from playing videogames on company time.

Interestingly, in a survey by *Forbes*, 69 percent of users of *Pokémon GO* said they played the game while at work, indicating the level of boredom many of us face at work in our daily lives.[35] While playing *Pokémon GO* at work is not going to change the world, the anti-work appropriation of gamification on workers' terms should be celebrated. The widespread adoption of smartphones has meant that many workers have found ways to access videogames away from the electronic supervision of their work computer. *Pokémon GO* was clearly able to capitalize on this anti-work sentiment, as the augmented reality (AR) mobile game was downloaded over 100 million times on Google Play and generated $200 million in sales. Nintendo's share price initially soared. Although, amusingly, it later dived as investors realized the company itself would not profit that much from the game, given it was developed by Niantic (and draws on data from Google, who also incubated the company). Presumably, investors had not checked this in advance.

There is also evidence that the refusal of work in relation to videogames is going beyond work avoidance in the workplace. David Graeber has observed that many people in the Global North are now working what they call "bullshit jobs."[36] As Jane McGonigal has explained: "Games provide a sense of waking in the morning with one goal: I'm trying to improve this skill, teammates are counting on me, and my online community is relying on me. There is a routine and daily progress that does a good job at replacing traditional work."[37] There is now evidence that in the US, a segment of young men are dropping out of the labor force to play videogames. Although this might sound surprising, "in some ways, the increase in video game time for men makes sense: Median wages for men have been stagnant for decades. Over the same period, the quality of video games has grown significantly."[38] The possibilities of videogame play offer far more than precarious, minimum-wage employment, in the case of aspiring Twitch broadcasters. Here it is worth returning to a reflection by Huizinga:

> It sometimes happens, however, that the spoil-sports in their turn make a new community with rules of its own. The outlaw, the revolutionary, the cabbalist or member of a secret society, indeed heretics of all kinds are of a highly associative if not sociable disposition, and a certain element of play is prominent in all their doings.[39]

While these were not dynamics that Huizinga was celebrating, we can see how they can be important for the development of an anti-work subjectivity. While there is a risk that this activity remains individualized, the social elements of many contemporary videogames provide a potentially collective route in these moments of resistance and play.

ONLINE PLAY

The social aspect has become key to understanding contemporary videogames. While some of those discussed above can be played offline, online play is incredibly important for understanding the culture. Things have moved a long way since players sat in front of the television to play *GoldenEye* with friends.

Massively multiplayer online role-playing games (MMORPGs) provide new and persistent online spaces for players. Take, for example, *World of Warcraft*, which was released in 2001 and has had over a hundred million accounts registered. It provides an online world in which players can fight, quest, level up, and collect items. In addition to these core features, players can train in professions, sell their creations and excess items, and form player-run guilds. The gameplay therefore "contains tropes that are immediately recognizable as capitalist structures, as the mechanics and aesthetics often mimic and reflect societal structures."[1] The game *EVE Online* similarly emphasizes player-driven economies and entails tales of intrigue, manipulation, betrayal, and so on.

Perhaps it is no surprise that these videogames broadly reproduce the structures of capitalism, but they also allow players to experiment within these systems, breaking away from the monotony of work (briefly, or for much longer periods). Within these systems, as the game genre's name suggests, players can role-play, meaning other players may not know their particular identity. These kinds of videogames are increasingly being replaced with shorter, more competitive experiences. Whether played on a console or PC, these games are often team-based competitions, requiring communication between players that is deeply shaped by the dynamics of oppression at play in the larger society.

The genres of MOBA (multiplayer online battle arena) games, along with competitive FPS videogames like *Counter-Strike*, are key to understanding these dynamics. MOBAs like *League of Legends* or *Dota 2*—which began as fan-made mods—are played over short rounds, usually around thirty minutes. While I had played *Counter-Strike* since I was a teenager, I only played *League of Legends* more recently. The experience of trying to learn is revealing. The five versus five team structure means that each person on the team needs to perform effectively to secure a victory. In contrast to the continuing progression of characters in MMORPGs, every player character in MOBAs starts each match from the beginning, so early mistakes can cause the other team to surge ahead. There is a close reliance on teamwork to win, where a failure by one player can ruin the experience (or the win-rate statistics) for the teammates. This sets the stage for a deeply competitive environment, one in which mistakes are quickly called out. This also means that players can vent their frustration by throwing a game—for example, deliberately dying and thereby "feeding" the opposing team with experience and gold.

As a new player, I was joining a game with an estimated highpoint of 100 million monthly players.[2] Before starting, I was warned by other people about the "toxic community" one encounters playing *League of Legends*. In my first session, I played only with bots (computer-controlled players). It seemed easy at that point, and with my four friendly bots, we easily won the game. After some experimentation, I decided it was time to try playing online. As the game loaded, other players started calling out positions. *League of Legends* has a complex meta-game, or "meta," which is essentially "the game of playing the game." Through the meta, the players determine their respective roles. They refer to a map, which is divided into three lanes—"top," "mid," and "bot," with an additional player as support for "bot," and yet another player roaming in the "jungle." In the version I played, the players can call out their preference. Two other players called "mid" and "bot," so I decided to go "top." Unfortunately, another player then decided to go "top" as well, which would put the distribution out of balance. We then ran into the same dilemma regarding the "mid" lane. However, after a torrent of abuse among the players, we came to a resolution. I moved into the "jungle," realizing I did not even have the first idea of what I should have been doing. The team rapidly collapsed into infighting and we lost.

I decided that further research would definitely be needed before playing again. *League of Legends* is both tactically and strategically complex, with a frequently changing meta. The process of learning to play is stressful; you are forced to contend with the game mechanics, the 137 different characters, the player-constituted meta, opposing players, and often your own team. The streaming platform Twitch provides a way to watch experienced and successful players, something that has become a resource for aspiring players. The main lesson from my experience is that it takes substantial effort to learn how to play. In an intensified process of competition, Caillois's *agôn* is clearly at work here.[3] This leads to the formation of expert communities with a high barrier to entry.

It can be a rewarding experience to compete and win with a team that works together. However, the *League of Legends* community does have incredibly toxic elements, and the playing experience is frequently damaged by players who throw the game because of some minor infraction by a teammate, or who use sexist or racist slurs, pouring bile into the back-and-forth.

To make sense of this contradictory experience of online play, it is worth returning again to the history of videogames. This is a history in which "there were women game makers and girl players. Yet despite this, the history of hackers, *manga* artists, and game developers is mainly a tale of men and boys."[4] Carol Shaw, who was the first female videogame developer at Atari, has reflected on the early gendering of the medium: "We never really discussed who our target demographic was. We didn't discuss gender or age. We just did games we thought would be fun."[5]

However, the fact that there was a lack of explicit discussion about gender did not mean that these were egalitarian workplaces. For example, Ray Kassar, before going on to be the CEO of Atari, once said in front of Shaw, "Gee, now that Atari has a female game designer, she can do interior decorating and cosmetic color-matching games!" Shaw noted that after he left the room, the other developers said: "Don't pay attention to him. Just do whatever you want." So whether or not videogames were deliberately gendered at this point, the general sexism in society still operated in the production process.

This early period of the videogames industry changed with the crisis that embroiled Atari in the 1980s, when Nintendo chose to shift toward the marketing of videogames through toy culture. This required systematic marketing analysis, and for the first time, "companies like Nintendo aggressively sought out people who played their games." They discovered that "more boys were playing video games than girls," and as a result, "video games were about to be reinvented."[6] Videogame marketing and advertising became increasingly gendered—one obvious example is Nintendo's decision to name its handheld videogame console the "Game Boy." It was also evident in the way videogame protagonists and characters were advertised. Ian Bogost argues that Nintendo's shift in the 1980s was a first key step that set the stage for "what we now call 'dude-bro' games happening in the early '90s."[7] A 1998 ad that Sony ran for the PlayStation serves as an example of this second phase:

> A grown man sits in a movie theater with his girlfriend. She's nagging him in an almost cartoonish way. Crash Bandicoot, from the PS1 game of the same name, is soon patrolling the theater, shining a flashlight on the man and telling him, "You are so totally whipped." A busty Lara Croft appears next to him, and he's given the choice of going home with his girlfriend, who is still nagging, or taking Lara Croft. He chooses the latter. The commercial ends with the tagline: "Live in your world. Play in ours."[8]

This kind of marketing has shaped the consumption of video-games today—who wants to play them, what makes video-games "popular," and what kind of projects get funding. Highly sexualized and objectifying depictions of women have become common in videogames. Interestingly, according to one study of videogame reviews, "reviewers mention such depictions rarely, but it is unclear why."[9]

The implications of the sexist gendering of videogames, along with deeply problematic representations of race, sexuality, and so on, are important to consider given that many videogame players today are young people. As noted by Monica K. Miller and Alicia Summers, because videogames "have the potential to influence the behaviors and attitudes of America's youth, it is important to recognize the messages these media present."[10] In the US and beyond, the "portrayal of males as powerful and muscular and females as attractive, sexy and helpless has implications for self-esteem and body image in both males and females." These portrayals have been critiqued in various ways by "identifying, exploring and bringing into focus stereotypical representations of gender."[11] The choice to market videogames to a particular demographic, mainly young men and boys, has involved reproducing these stereotypes. Critiques are necessary because they can highlight that this marketing strategy is a choice, and in the process "challenge stereotypes of gender because ultimately, there is no innate, natural link between gender and sex, yet culture has imposed a hierarchy of roles based on these social, gendered constructs."[12]

This opening-up of videogame culture to questions of representation has occurred alongside a broader recognition that it is not just young white men who play videogames. The popular notion that "girls don't play games" has "less to do with the actual numbers of players as much as it has to do with an idea that was heavily circulated from the '90s through television commercials, magazine ads, video game box art and the media."[13] This recognition of a wider audience has also started to change how videogames are marketed, in turn influencing the direction that the next generation of games can take.

For many players, this gendering of videogames comes to the fore when they go online. Online play has become a key part of many videogame experiences. However, not everyone has a similar experience when they go online. With any major online title, from *Counter-Strike* to *League of Legends*, it is easy for players to experience interactions that are toxic and often loaded with sexism. Although this phenomenon has complex roots—and is in part a product of the history of gameplay noted above—the anonymity of online play, along with that of associated forums, has provided a place where this toxic culture can grow. The clearest example of this is the Gamergate movement. It began on 8chan, a website where sexual and racist slurs are common and "swearing close to mandatory." Trolling is also prevalent, as are more extreme methods like "doxing"—finding and publishing private or identifying material about someone.[14] This movement left the forums and developed into an online harassment campaign through the hashtag #GamerGate, targeting game developers Zoë Quinn and Brianna Wu, feminist media critic Anita Sarkeesian, and many others, including academics.[15] As the campaign escalated, forms of harassment started, including doxing, threats of sexual violence, and death threats. In 2014, it became covered more widely in the media, which began to discuss a "culture war" taking place over videogames.[16]

The "Gamergaters" thus formed a virtual mob, directed against alternative voices, criticism, and new forms of representation in videogames. That Gamergate transpired highlights that "playing games is not an isolated event."[17] While these events made little sense to people outside of videogames, they did make sense to some of the people on the periphery of the industry. For example, Steve Bannon, who helped to run *Breitbart News* and then joined the Trump administration, developed a close knowledge of gamer culture through his involvement in the *World of Warcraft* gold-mining company Internet Gaming Entertainment (IGE).[18] The company employed

Chinese workers to grind through repetitive tasks to earn in-game money and items, which would then be sold to wealthier players, mainly in the US. As Joshua Green has argued, Bannon's time at IGE

> introduced him to a hidden world, burrowed deep into his psyche, and provided a kind of conceptual framework that he would later draw on to build up the audience for *Breitbart News*, and then to help marshal the online armies of trolls and activists that overran national politicians and helped give rise to Donald Trump.[19]

While there has been a rise of reactionary politics on the internet more broadly, commentators like Matt Lees have noted that "the similarities between Gamergate and the far-right online movement, the 'alt-right,' are huge, startling and in no way a coincidence."[20] There are clear and concrete links between the alt-right and Gamergate; they are coming together, not just out of a shared interest, but because they are being marshaled into a right-wing political force.

The players of videogames operate within complex and developed cultures that emerge directly from videogames, as well as from the act of collectively playing them. The massification of videogame play has meant, perhaps, a loss of the isolated "gamer" identity. However, the notion of a "gamer" identity has developed within the culture(s) of videogame play and is, in part, the result of a struggle—one that the left, broadly speaking, lost. This failure also has an impact beyond just play, feeding back into the work conditions for those who make videogames. In a recent example, two writers for the popular online game *Guild Wars 2* were fired by the developer ArenaNet after responding to online harassment. One of the writers, Jessica Price, tweeted: "Today in being a female game dev: 'Allow me—a person who does not work with you—explain to you how you do your job.'" She then followed up with another tweet: "Since we've got a lot of hurt manfeels today, lemme make something clear: this is my feed. I'm not on the clock here. I'm not your emotional courtesan just because I'm a dev. Don't expect me to pretend to like you here." Another writer defended her, and ArenaNet responded by stating: "Recently two of our employees failed to uphold our standards of communicating with players. As a result, they're no longer with the company."[21] Rather than supporting its workers, the chose to give in to the online harassment and set a precedent that the players could do what they wanted. No doubt, many other developers in the industry saw this chain of events and nervously thought about what they have written or said online.

This is the context in which people participate in online video-game play. Young male players are able to engage in competition against players across the world without fear of harassment or unfair treatment because of their gender. This can lead up to the possibility of entering professionalized esports competitions, with increasing rewards and fame. This is a far departure from the guiding spirit behind the first multiplayer online games, then known as MUDs (multi-user dungeons). Creator Richard Bartle envisioned that multiplayer videogames start from the position that "everyone starts off on an equal footing in this artificial world." Creating them was a "political gesture," he explained:

> The original hacker ethic was, you can do what you like as long as you don't hurt anyone else. That fed into games and it has propagated outwards. The more games you play the more sense you have of things like fairness—if you play an unfair game it's no fun, it's not a good game. I think that makes you more resistant to examples of unfairness in the real world. You may start to think, why shouldn't gay people get married, what the hell, it doesn't affect me?[22]

Online videogames have developed significantly since Bartle was experimenting and hacking in the 1970s. That vision of on-line play he describes would seem quite jarring to anyone who has recently played *Counter-Strike*, *League of Legends*, or many other examples, where the gameplay is often accompanied by a torrent of verbal abuse, shouted into microphones by other players. Removed from customary social constraints, players say things that we would hope they would think twice about in other social environments. The rise of the alt-right has provided an opportunity for this kind of toxicity to escape the confines of the game, seeping into society. Referring to his creations, Richard Bartle said he hoped that "some of the culture that came out of games has affected the real world," but this was certainly not the kind of example he had in mind.

The dynamics of oppression that have been discussed here remain an unavoidable part of online videogame play. If online videogames are to provide the kind of space that Bartle discussed, that is something that needs to be fought for as hard as any round of *Counter-Strike* or *League of Legends*.

CONCLUSION: WHY VIDEOGAMES MATTER

So why should Marxists be interested in videogames? The first reason is that videogames are not simply some diversion, or opium of the people, but a complex cultural commodity. Marxists should be interested in videogames because their production, circulation, and consumption can provide important insights into the inner workings of contemporary capitalism. Play and games, regrettably, are not usually the subject of Marxist analysis. Marxists tend to be interested in the shape and dynamics of capitalism, or sometimes—and often not enough—in workers themselves, and their resistance and organization. Owing to the supposed frivolity or "unproductive" nature of play, it does not usually fit within either of these lines of analysis.

Within the history of videogames, however, it is possible to see moments of resistance and opposition right from the start. In the US, computers and the new workers who could program them were put to work planning missile launches and doomsday scenarios, but workers found ways to hack these computers to design anti-work diversions that became the first videogames. At this point, the possibility of a modern videogames industry must have seemed quite unlikely, but a process of "escape and capture" by capitalism soon unfolded. That initial hacker impulse, increasingly understood now as playbour, remains an integral part of the industry. From the early games to the mods of *Half-Life* and

Warcraft, there has always been a hard-to-control element that escapes and that capital attempts to capture.

The production of videogames today involves "the highly disciplined and exploitative control of its cognitariat workforce—increasingly prominent in cognitive capitalism generally."[1] In these pages, we identified new ways companies manage and exploit workers in the games studio, but we also explored the essential global supply chains that mix both material and immaterial production. As Ian Williams has argued, the "exploitation in the video game industry provides a glimpse at how the rest of us may be working in years to come."[2] We discussed this kind of work through *Notes from Below*'s class composition framework, understood as "a material relation with three parts: the first is the organisation of labour power into a working class (technical composition); the second is the organisation of the working class into a class society (social composition); the third is the self-organisation of the working class into a force for class struggle (political composition)."[3]

This allowed us to unpack the organization of videogame work. The first key finding is that the technical composition remains a challenge for capital, as this kind of labor process is very difficult to manage. The result is a widespread use of crunch time—working very long hours, especially toward the end of a project. The second is that the social composition needs to be understood in terms of equality—and particularly gender. The experiences of institutional sexism, along with crunch time, represent two factors that are currently provoking a political recomposition. The latest wave of worker organizing, with Game Workers Unite, is an incredibly exciting development. This not to say that the videogames industry is the most important sector of contemporary capitalism, but its dynamics are important to unpack and understand. As Nick Dyer-Witheford and Greig de Peuter have argued: "Virtual games are one molecular component of this undecidable collective mutation, which is revolutionizing life from the mines to the metaverse. In that sense, they are games with worlds to win."[4]

This leads to the second reason that Marxists should be interested in videogames. Videogames are an incredibly popular cultural form, with huge numbers of players across the world. While a cursory glance at videogames may pick out the worst content, as many games "tend to a reactionary imperial content, as militarized, marketized, entertainment commodities," there is another side to consider. Games also "tend to a radical, multitudinous form, as collaborative, constructive, experimental digital productions."[5] This is why the connections of the videogames industry with the military-industrial complex figured into my discussion. These deep links have endured, intensifying as the military has directly and indirectly intervened in the production of games, with this relationship now also shaping the military in return. This accelerating feedback loop stands as a metaphor, defining the contours between technological innovation and the organization of work in late capitalism.

There is a struggle over what kinds of videogames we play and how we play them, as well as a struggle between labor and capital in the process of actually producing them. Videogames can therefore "also serve a critical purpose, introducing uncomfortable facts, unmasking social foibles, encouraging oppositions, and even presenting alternative futures. This, too, emerges from their history. Games, like science fiction, often provide the cover for fundamental criticism and even revolt."[6] If the alt-right and Gamergate have weaponized videogames and their communities as political tools, the best response, to apply Walter Benjamin's words from a different context, is "to politicize art."[7] Marxists should therefore be concerned with videogames. To quote Stuart Hall once again, regarding the significance of popular culture:

> Popular culture is one of the sites where this struggle for and against a culture of the powerful is engaged: it is also the stake to be won or lost in that struggle. It is the arena of consent and resistance. It is partly where hegemony arises, and where it is secured. It is not a sphere where socialism, a socialist culture—already fully formed—might be simply "expressed." But it is one of the places where socialism might

be constituted. That is why "popular culture" matters. Otherwise, to tell you the truth, I don't give a damn about it.[8]

So, if Marxists should be interested in videogames, why, then, should people interested in videogames care about what Marxism has to say? Marxist criticism of videogames is not intended to condemn videogames as some sort of bourgeois form that recreates the worst of capitalism. Yes, many videogames have problematic themes and have oppression written into them from the start. But this is also true of novels, television, film, and life itself. Despite the fact that "many people have a difficulty differentiating cultural criticism from censorship,"[9] it is possible to criticize videogames while still playing and enjoying them. A Marxist analysis draws out the radical history of videogames, placing them within a complex history of hackers and corporations, escape and co-option, resistance and oppression. A focus on the work of production draws back the veil that obscures how we end up with the kinds of games that we play. This can reveal much about the way our games are made, but also can shed light on the kinds of work that we have to do under capitalism. Games can be both an escape from work and a potential way to experiment and explore an alternative to the society that we have now. If videogame workers can find new ways to organize under capitalism in the absence of a history of strong workers' organization or traditions of trade unionism, then many other workers can find inspiration too. Workers' inquiry can be the first step toward doing this.

There is also a clear shared interest for Marxists and people who play videogames. Videogames make an intervention into the world. They bring together huge numbers of people through shared activities, building new communities and cultures. While the early developers may have dreamed of the progressive possibilities of videogames, the reality has become much darker. From Gamergate to the alt-right, we can no longer ignore videogames as a field of cultural struggle. This does not call for censoring videogames, but rather for understanding that battles of ideas are won and lost on this terrain. There is much to be celebrated with videogame culture. It is one that I have grown up around and share with many friends. However, as Leigh Alexander has argued, "when you decline to create or to curate a culture in your spaces, you're responsible for what spawns in the vacuum. That's what's been happening to games."[10] Failing to take on those struggles has meant the left—with a few brilliant exceptions—has effectively vacated that battle for ideas.

At present, fighting for a better online culture or contesting the toxicity of some videogames seems like a particularly daunting task. For an individual player, it surely is. However, the histories of resistance and struggles in the field of videogames show that this has not been a story with only one side. Struggle has been a part of videogames since their inception. This is something the left, Marxists, and videogame players need to take up again. What is different in this moment is the emergence of a workers' movement in the videogames industry. Anyone who wants a more progressive online culture, a broader range of videogames, and full knowledge about how the people who made them were treated should support Game Workers Unite. They have the potential to not only reshape the work of videogames but also transform the kinds of videogames we get, as well as how we play them.

Returning once more to *Assassin's Creed Syndicate*, there is a moment in the game when the virtual Marx gives the player the "challenge" to "help those who *really* need your assistance. The working people." In real life, Marx laid out another challenge— that of helping the working people through workers' inquiry.[11] This was a process of connecting the experiences and struggles of workers with revolutionary change. His ideas of workers' inquiry of course need to be updated, and hopefully this book can contribute to this. Organizing at work is the key way that we can change the world, but that does not mean we should do so while leaving the dominant ideas in society unchallenged. Taking videogames seriously as part of this struggle is no longer something the left can ignore. The command that *Assassin's Creed* gives the player remains an important starting point: "Follow Marx."

NOTES

Author's Note

1   Jamie Woodcock, "The Work of Play: Marx and the Video Games Industry in the United Kingdom," *Journal of Gaming and Virtual Worlds* 8, no. 2 (2016): 131–43.

Introduction

Epigraph source: Stuart Hall, "Notes on Deconstructing 'the Popular,'" in *People's History and Socialist Theory*, ed. Raphael Samuel (London: Routledge & Kegan Paul, 1981), 239.

1   Brian Crecente, "Nearly 70% of Americans Play Video Games, Mostly on Smartphones (Study)," *Variety*, September 11, 2018, https://variety .com/2018/gaming/news/how-many-people-play-games-in-the -u-s-1202936332; SuperData, "2017 Year in Review: Digital Games and Interactive Media" (SuperData Research Holdings, 2018).

2   Karl Marx, "A Workers' Inquiry," *New International* 4, no. 12 (1938).

3   "Karl Marx vs Meyer," Chessgames, www.chessgames.com/perl /chessgame?gid=1278768.

A History of Videogames and Play

1   See Jamie Woodcock (@jamie_woodcock), "Academic writing question: which term do you prefer?," Twitter, May 14, 2018.

2   Quoted in Chris Kohler, "On 'Videogame' Versus 'Video Game,'" *Wired*, November 12, 2007.

3   "Game Definitions," Molleindustria, http://www.gamedefinitions.com/#.

4   Nicolas Esposito, "A Short and Simple Definition of What a Videogame Is," Proceedings of DiGRA 2005 Conference: Changing Views – Worlds in Play, 2005; italics in the original.

5   Jesper Juul, "Introduction to Game Time," in *First Person*, eds. Noah Wardrip-Fruin and Pat Harrigan (Cambridge, MA: MIT Press, 2004), 140.

6   Richard Rouse, *Game Design* (Sudbury, MA: Wordware Publishing, 2004), xx.

7   Mark Fisher, *Capitalist Realism: Is There No Alternative?* (Winchester: Zero Books, 2009).

8   Johan Huizinga, *Homo Ludens: A Study of the Play-Element in Culture* (Kettering, OH: Angelico Press, 2006), 1.

9   Huizinga, *Homo Ludens*, 9.

10   *Notes from Below* editors, "The Workers' Inquiry and Social Composition," *Notes from Below*, January 29, 2018, www.notesfrombelow .org/article/workers-inquiry-and-social-composition.

11   Huizinga, *Homo Ludens*, 13.

12   Katie Salen and Eric Zimmerman, *Rules of Play: Game Design Fundamentals* (Cambridge, MA: MIT Press, 2003), 94.

13   Edward Castronova, *Synthetic Worlds: The Business and Culture of Online Games* (Chicago, IL: University of Chicago Press, 2005), 147.

14   Salen and Zimmerman, *Rules of Play*, 95.

15   Nick Dyer-Witheford and Greig de Peuter, *Games of Empire: Global Capitalism and Video Games* (Minneapolis and London: University of Minnesota Press, 2009), xxxiv.

16   Roger Caillois, *Man, Play and Games* (Urbana and Chicago: University of Illinois Press, 2001), 5–6.

17   Caillois, *Man, Play and Games*, 9–10.

18   Caillois, *Man, Play and Games*, 12, 13.

19   Lars Kristensen and Ulf Wilhelmsson, "Roger Caillois and Marxism: A Game Studies Perspective," *Games and Culture* 12, no. 4 (2017): 388.

20   Kristensen and Wilhelmsson, "Roger Caillois and Marxism," 388.

21   Kristensen and Wilhelmsson, "Roger Caillois and Marxism," 393.

22   Marshall McLuhan, *Understanding Media: The Extensions of Man* (London: Routledge, 2001), 258.

23   McLuhan, *Understanding Media*, 259.

24   "Video Game History Timeline," National Museum of Play, www .museumofplay.org/about/icheg/video-game-history/timeline.

25   Claude E. Shannon, "Programming a Computer for Playing Chess," *Philosophical Magazine* 41, no. 314 (1950).

26   Dyer-Witheford and de Peuter, *Games of Empire*, xxix.

27   Dyer-Witheford and de Peuter, *Games of Empire*, 7.

28   "Video Game History Timeline."

29   "Video Game History Timeline."

30   "Video Game History Timeline."

31   Dyer-Witheford and de Peuter, *Games of Empire*, 7.

32   Dyer-Witheford and de Peuter, *Games of Empire*, 7.

33   Dyer-Witheford and de Peuter, *Games of Empire*, 8.

34   Dyer-Witheford and de Peuter, *Games of Empire*, 9.

35   Dyer-Witheford and de Peuter, *Games of Empire*, 9.

36   Dyer-Witheford and de Peuter, *Games of Empire*, 8.

37   "Video Game History Timeline."

38   "Video Game History Timeline."

39   Martin Gardner, "Mathematical Games: The Fantastic Combinations
       of John Conway's New Solitaire Game 'Life,'" *Scientific American* 223
       (1970): 120–23.
40   "Video Game History Timeline."
41   "Video Game History Timeline."
42   Dyer-Witheford and de Peuter, *Games of Empire*, 11.
43   Dyer-Witheford and de Peuter, *Games of Empire*, 12.
44   John J. Anderson, "Dave Tells Ahl: The History of Creative Computing,"
       Creative Computing 10, no. 11 (1984).
45   "AtGames to Launch Atari Flashback® 4 to Celebrate Atari's 40th
       Anniversary!" iReach, last modified November 12, 2012, www
       .ireachcontent.com/news-releases/atgames-to-launch-atari-flashback-4
       -to-celebrate-ataris-40th-anniversary-178903531.html?c=y.
46   Quoted in Keith Stuart, "Richard Bartle: We Invented Multiplayer
       Games as a Political Gesture," *Guardian*, November 17, 2014,
       http://www.theguardian.com/technology/2014/nov/17/richard
       -bartle-multiplayer-games-political-gesture.
47   Stuart, "Richard Bartle."
48   Quoted in Stuart, "Richard Bartle."
49   Stephen Kline, Nick Dyer-Witheford, and Greig de Peuter, *Digital
       Play: The Interaction of Technology, Culture, and Marketing* (Montreal and
       Kingston: McGill-Queen's University Press, 2003), 96.
50   "Video Game History Timeline."
51   Dyer-Witheford and de Peuter, *Games of Empire*, 13.
52   Daniel Joseph, "Code of Conduct: Platforms Are Taking over Capitalism,
       but Code Convenes Class Struggle as Well as Control," *Real Life*, April
       12, 2017, http://reallifemag.com/code-of-conduct.
53   Dyer-Witheford and de Peuter, *Games of Empire*, 13.
54   Mary Aitken, *The Cyber Effect: A Pioneering Cyberpsychologist Explains How
       Human Behaviour Changes Online* (London: John Murray, 2016).
55   Drew Robarge, "From Landfill to Smithsonian Collections: 'E.T. the
       Extra-Terrestrial' Atari 2600 Game," *Smithsonian*, December 15, 2014,
       http://americanhistory.si.edu/blog/landfill-smithsonian
       -collections-et-extra-terrestrial-atari-2600-game.
56   Dyer-Witheford and de Peuter, *Games of Empire*, 14.
57   Dyer-Witheford and de Peuter, *Games of Empire*, 14.
58   Dyer-Witheford and de Peuter, *Games of Empire*, 15.
59   Dal Yong Jin, *Korea's Online Gaming Empire* (Cambridge, MA: MIT Press,
       2010).
60   Dyer-Witheford and de Peuter, *Games of Empire*, 16.
61   Nintendo, "Historical Data: Consolidated Sales Transition by Region,"
       last modified October 26, 2017, https://web.archive.org/web
       /20171026163943/https://www.nintendo.co.jp/ir/finance/historical
       _data/xls/consolidated_sales_e1703.xlsx.
62   Joseph, "Code of Conduct."

63   Nintendo, "Historical Data."
64   Emily Gera, "This Is How Tetris Wants You to Celebrate for Its 30th Anniversary," *Polygon*, May 21, 2014, www.polygon.com/2014 /5/21/5737488/tetris-turns-30-alexey-pajitnov.
65   "Yearly Market Report," *Famitsu Weekly*, June 21, 1996.
66   Nintendo, "Historical Data."
67   "Video Game History Timeline."
68   Sony Computer Entertainment, "PlayStation Cumulative Production Shipments of Hardware," May 24, 2011, https://web.archive.org/web /20110524023857/http://www.scei.co.jp/corporate/data/bizdataps _e.html.
69   Nintendo, "Historical Data."
70   "Video Game History Timeline."
71   Dyer-Witheford and de Peuter, *Games of Empire*, 20.
72   Sony Computer Entertainment, "PlayStation 2 Worldwide Hardware Unit Sales," November 1, 2013, https://web.archive.org/web /20131101120621/http://www.scei.co.jp/corporate/data/bizdataps2 _sale_e.html.
73   Nintendo, "Historical Data."
74   Colin Moriarty, "Vita Sales Are Picking Up Thanks to PS4 Remote Play," *IGN*, November 17, 2014, http://uk.ign.com/articles/2014/11/17/vita -sales-are-picking-up-thanks-to-ps4-remote-play.
75   Xbox.com, "Gamers Catch Their Breath as Xbox 360 and Xbox Live Reinvent Next-Generation Gaming," May 10, 2006, https://web .archive.org/web/20070709062832/http://www.xbox.com/zh-SG /community/news/2006/20060510.htm.
76   Eddie Makuch, "E3 2014: $399 Xbox One Out Now, Xbox 360 Sales Rise to 84 million," *GameSpot*, June 9, 2014, https://web.archive .org/web/20141013194652/http://www.gamespot.com/articles/e3 -2014-399-xbox-one-out-now-xbox-360-sales-rise-to-84-million /1100-6420231/.
77   "Video Game History Timeline."
78   Sony Computer Entertainment, "Q4 FY2014 Consolidated Financial Results Forecast (Three Months Ended March 31, 2015)," April 30, 2015, www.sony.net/SonyInfo/IR/financial/fr/14q4_sonypre.pdf.
79   Nintendo, "Historical Data."
80   "Video Game History Timeline."
81   "Video Game History Timeline."
82   Nintendo, "Historical Data."
83   "Dedicated Video Game Sales Units," Nintendo, January 31, 2018, www.nintendo.co.jp/ir/en/finance/hard_soft/index.html.
84   Aernout, "Minecraft Sales Reach 144 Million Across all Platforms; 74 Million Monthly Players," *Wccftech*, January 22, 2018, https://wccftech .com/minecraft-sales-144-million/.

85 Eugene Kim, "Amazon Buys Twitch for $970 Million in Cash," *Business Insider*, August 25, 2014, www.businessinsider.com/amazon -buys-twitch-2014-8.

86 Craig Smith, "50 Interesting Fortnite Stats and Facts (November 2018) by the Numbers," *DMR*, November 17, 2018, https:// expandedramblings.com/index.php/fortnite-facts-and-statistics/.

The Videogames Industry

1   Maurizio Lazzarato, "Immaterial Labour," in *Radical Thought in Italy*, eds. Paolo Virno and Michael Hardt (Minneapolis: University of Minnesota Press, 1996).

2   Nick Dyer-Witheford, *Cyber-Proletariat: Global Labour in the Digital Vortex* (London: Pluto, 2015), 42.

3   SuperData, "2017 Year in Review: Digital Games and Interactive Media" (SuperData Research Holdings, 2018).

4   SuperData, "Year in Review," 5.

5   SuperData, "Year in Review," 9–10.

6   SuperData, "Year in Review," 13.

7   SuperData, "Year in Review," 19.

8   Stephen E. Siwek, "Video Games in the 21st Century," Entertainment Software Association, 2017.

9   Ukie, "The Games Industry in Numbers," Ukie, http://ukie.org.uk/research.

10 Ukie, "The Games Industry in Numbers."

11 Ukie, "The Games Industry in Numbers."

12 Boris Johnson, "The Writing Is on the Wall – Computer Games Rot the Brain," *Telegraph*, December 28, 2006, www.telegraph.co.uk/comment /personal-view/3635699/The-writing-is-on-the-wall-computer-games -rot-the-brain.html.

13 Tom Phillips, "Disgraced Senator Who Campaigned against Violent Video Games Jailed," *Eurogamer*, February 25, 2016, www.eurogamer.net /articles/2016-02-25-disgraced-senator-who-campaigned-against -violent-video-games-jailed.

14 Quoted in Julian Benson, "10 Years Ago, Boris Johnson Held Games Responsible for 'Ignorance, Underachievement and Poverty,'" Kotaku, January 19, 2016, www.kotaku.co.uk/2016/01/19/10-years-ago -boris-johnson-said-that-games-were-responsible-for-ignorance- underachievement-and-poverty.

15 Olsberg-SPI and Nordicity, "Economic Contribution of the UK's Film, High-End TV, Video Game, and Animation Programming Sectors," February 2015, www.bfi.org.uk/education-research/film-industry -statistics-reports/reports/uk-film-economy/economic-contribution -uks-film-sectors.

16 The Video Games Tax Relief program "allows video games studios to claim a cash repayment or tax relief from the Government after they have spent money on developing a video game." See "Video Games Tax Relief," Ukie, https://ukie.org.uk/a2f/VGTR.

17   Ukie, "The Games Industry in Numbers."
18   Olsberg-SPI and Nordicity, "Economic Contribution of the UK's Film," 52.
19   Juan Mateos-Garcia, Hasan Bakhshi, and Mark Lenel, *A Map of the UK Games Industry* (London: Nesta, 2014), 6.
20   Brendan Sinclair, "GTA V Dev Costs over $137 Million, Says Analyst," GamesIndustry.biz, February 1, 2013, www.gamesindustry.biz/articles/2013-02-01-gta-v-dev-costs-over-USD137-million-says-analyst.
21   Aphra Kerr, *The Business and Culture of Digital Games: Gamework/Gameplay* (London: Sage, 2006), 4.
22   Graham Kirkpatrick, *Computer Games and the Social Imaginary* (Cambridge: Polity, 2013), 109.
23   Paul Thompson, Rachel Parker, and Stephen Cox, "Labour and Asymmetric Power Relations in Global Value Chains: The Digital Entertainment Industries and Beyond," in *Putting Labour in its Place: Labour Process Analysis and Global Value Chains*, eds. Kirsty Newsome et al. (London: Palgrave, 2015), 57.
24   Kirkpatrick, *Computer Games and the Social Imaginary*, 117.
25   Mateos-Garcia, Bakhshi, and Lenel, *A Map of the UK Games Industry*, 4.
26   Olsberg-SPI and Nordicity, *Economic Contribution of the UK's Film*, 52.
27   Mateos-Garcia, Bakhshi, and Lenel, A Map of the UK Games Industry, 16.
28   Olsberg-SPI and Nordicity, "Economic Contribution of the UK's Film," 52.
29   Stephen E. Siwek, "Video Games in the 21st Century," Entertainment Software Association, 2017.
30   Olsberg-SPI and Nordicity, "Economic Contribution of the UK's Film," 58.
31   Paolo Ruffino, "Narrative of Independent Production in Video Game Culture," *Loading . . .* 7, no. 11 (2012).
32   Dyer-Witheford and de Peuter, *Games of Empire*, 66.
33   Niall McCarthy, "The Companies Making the Most from Video Games [Infographic]," *Forbes*, May 14, 2018, www.forbes.com/sites/niallmccarthy/2018/05/14/the-companies-making-the-most-from-video-games-infographic/#3c2c45a96610.
34   Jason Schreier, "Bungie Gets £75 Million for New Non-Destiny Game," Kotaku, June 1, 2018, www.kotaku.co.uk/2018/06/01/bungie-gets-100-million-for-new-non-destiny-game.
35   Karl Marx, *Capital: A Critique of Political Economy*, vol. 1 (London: Penguin Books, 1976), 125.
36   Marx, *Capital*, 249.
37   David B. Nieborg, "Prolonging the Magic: The Political Economy of the 7th Generation Console Game," *Eludamos: Journal for Computer Game Culture* 8, no. 1 (2014): 47–63.
38   The figures that follow come from UK but have been converted into the US dollar equivalent.

39   Keza MacDonald, "Why You Pay What You Pay for Video Games,"
     Kotaku, September 30, 2015, www.kotaku.co.uk/2015/09/30/why
     -you-pay-what-you-pay-for-video-games.
40   MacDonald, "Why You Pay What You Pay."
41   MacDonald, "Why You Pay What You Pay."
42   Quoted in MacDonald, "Why You Pay What You Pay."
43   MacDonald, "Why You Pay What You Pay."
44   SuperData report quoted in MacDonald, "Why You Pay What You Pay."
     Figures in US dollars have been converted from pounds sterling.
45   MacDonald, "Why You Pay What You Pay."
46   Nieborg, "Prolonging the Magic."
47   Nieborg, "Prolonging the Magic."
48   Julian Benson, "EA Makes Twice as Much from DLC as It Does from
     Selling Full Games Online," Kotaku, November 2, 2015, www.kotaku
     .co.uk/2015/11/02/ea-makes-twice-as-much-from-dlc-as-it-does-from
     -selling-full-games-online.
49   Nieborg, "Prolonging the Magic"; italics in the original.
50   Ian Bogost, *Unit Operations: An Approach to Videogame Criticism*
     (Cambridge, MA: MIT Press, 2006), 66.
51   Nieborg, "Prolonging the Magic"; italics in original.
52   Daniel Joseph, "Code of Conduct: Platforms Are Taking Over
     Capitalism, but Code Convenes Class Struggle as Well as Control," *Real
     Life*, April 12, 2017, http://reallifemag.com/code-of-conduct/.
53   Ben Kuchera, "Report: 7,672 Games Were Released on Steam in 2017,"
     Polygon, January 12, 2018, www.polygon.com/2018/1/10/16873446
     /steam-release-dates-2017.
54   Joseph, "Code of Conduct."
55   Nick Srnicek, *Platform Capitalism* (Cambridge: Polity, 2017), 43.
56   Joseph, "Code of Conduct."
57   Joseph, "Code of Conduct."
58   Joseph, "Code of Conduct."
59   Andy Chalk, "Valve and Perfect World Are Bringing Steam to China,"
     PC Gamer, June 11, 2018, www.pcgamer.com/valve-and
     -perfect-world-are-bringing-steam-to-china/.
60   Holger Pötzsch and Phil Hammond, "War/Game: Studying Relations
     between Violent Conflict, Games, and Play," *Game Studies* 16, no. 2 (2016).
61   See, for example, Ed Halter, *From Sun Tzu to Xbox: War and Video
     Games* (New York: Avalon Publishing Group, 2006); James Der Derian,
     Virtuous War: Mapping the Military-Industrial-Media-Entertainment Network
     (London: Routledge, 2009); Nina B. Huntemann and Matthew T. Payne,
     Joystick Soldiers: The Politics of Play in Military Video Games (London:
     Routledge, 2010); Gerald Voorhees, Joshua Call, and Katie Whitlock,
     Guns, Grenades, and *Grunts: First-Person Shooter Games* (New York:
     Bloomsbury, 2012); Corey Mead, *War Play: Video Games and the Future of
     Armed Conflict* (New York: Houghton Mifflin, 2013).

62   Nick Hopkins, "Ministry of Defence Forced to Update Its War Games for Xbox Generation," *Guardian*, December 28, 2011, www.theguardian.com/uk/2011/dec/28/ministry-defence-war-games-xbox.

63   Hopkins, "Ministry of Defence Forced."

64   Stephen Kline, Nick Dyer-Witheford, and Greig de Peuter, *Digital Play: The Interaction of Technology, Culture, and Marketing* (Montreal and Kingston: McGill-Queen's University Press, 2003), 99.

65   Michael Brooks, "If You Can Play a Video Game, You Can Fly a Drone," *New Statesman*, June 13, 2012, www.newstatesman.com/sci-tech/sci-tech/2012/06/play-video-game-fly-drone.

66   Matthew T. Payne, *Playing War: Military Video Games after 9/11* (New York: NYU Press, 2016), 6.

67   Kline, Dyer-Witheford, and de Peuter, *Digital Play*, 244.

68   Roger Stahl, *Militainment, Inc.: War, Media, and Popular Culture* (London: Routledge, 2010), 6.

69   Payne, *Playing War*, 6.

70   Quoted in Keith Stuart, "Call of Duty: Advanced Warfare: 'We Worked with a Pentagon Adviser,'" *Guardian*, August 28, 2014, www.theguardian.com/technology/2014/aug/28/call-of-duty-advanced-warfare-pentagon-adviser.

71   Stuart, "Call of Duty."

72   Strike Fighter Consulting, "About," Strike Fighter Consulting, 2011, http://strikefighterconsultinginc.com/about/.

73   Dabney B., "Did the DoD Forever Change the FPS Video Game Industry?," Strike Fighter Consulting, November 9, 2012, http://strikefighterconsultinginc.com/blog/did-the-dod-forever-change-the-video-game-industry/.

74   Strike Fighter Consulting, "About"; Dabney B., "Did the DoD Forever Change?"

75   Simon Parkin, "Shooters: How Video Games Fund Arms Manufacturers," *Eurogamer*, January 31, 2013, www.eurogamer.net/articles/2013-02-01-shooters-how-video-games-fund-arms-manufacturers.

76   Quoted in Parkin, "Shooters."

77   Parkin, "Shooters."

78   Parkin, "Shooters."

79   Jamie Doward, "Does UK's Lucrative Arms Trade Come at the Cost of Political Repression?," *Guardian*, February 12, 2017, www.theguardian.com/world/2017/feb/12/british-arms-deals-with-saudi-arabia-high-court.

80   Parkin, "Shooters."

81   Quoted in Parkin, "Shooters."

82   Simon Parkin, "Call of Duty: Gaming's Role in the Military-Entertainment Complex," *Guardian*, October 22, 2014, www.theguardian.com/technology/2014/oct/22/call-of-duty-gaming-role-military-entertainment-complex.

The Work of Videogames

1   Ryan Davis, "Game Dev Story Review," Giant Bomb, November 2, 2010, www.giantbomb.com/reviews/game-dev-story-review/1900-336.

2   Jason Schreier, "What's Right (and Wrong) with Game Dev Story's Addictive Simulation," *Wired*, December 3, 2010, www.wired.com/2010/12/game-dev-story.

3   Rick Lane, "A Conspiracy of Silence: How NDAs Are Harming the Games Industry," Kotaku, January 25, 2016, www.kotaku.co.uk/2016/01/25/a-conspiracy-of-silence-how-ndas-are-harming-the-games-industry.

4   Stephen Totilo, "A Price of Games Journalism," Kotaku, November 19, 2015, https://kotaku.com/a-price-of-games-journalism-1743526293.

5   Quoted in Lane, "A Conspiracy of Silence."

6   Lane, "A Conspiracy of Silence."

7   Lane, "A Conspiracy of Silence."

8   Marx, *Capital*, 279–80.

9   Marx, *Capital*.

10 Friedrich Engels, *The Condition of the Working Class in England* (Oxford: Oxford University Press, 2009).

11 David Harvey, *A Companion to Marx's Capital* (London: Verso, 2010), 141.

12 Marx, *Capital*, 397.

13 Harry Cleaver, *Reading Capital Politically* (Brighton, UK: Harvester Press, 1979), 20.

14 Michael A. Lebowitz, *Following Marx: Method, Critique and Crisis* (Boston: Brill, 2009), 314.

15 Lebowitz, *Following Marx*, 310, 314.

16 Karl Marx, "A Workers' Inquiry," *New International* 4, no. 12 (1938): 379.

17 Marx, "A Workers' Inquiry," 379.

18 Cleaver, *Reading Capital Politically*, 58.

19 Jamie Woodcock, "The Workers' Inquiry from Trotskyism to Operaismo: A Political Methodology for Investigating the Workplace," *Ephemera* 14, no. 3 (2014): 493–513.

20 Jamie Woodcock, *Working the Phones: Control and Resistance in Call Centres* (London: Pluto, 2017).

21 "Interview with Vittorio Rieser," *Generation Online*, October 3, 2001, www.generation-online.org/t/vittorio.htm.

22 *Notes from Below* editors, "The Workers' Inquiry and Social Composition," *Notes from Below* 1 (January 29, 2018), www.notesfrombelow.org/article/workers-inquiry-and-social-composition.

23 Julian Kücklich, "Precarious Playbour: Modders and the Digital Games Industry," *Fibreculture Journal* 5, no. 1 (2005).

24 Tiziana Terranova, "Free Labor: Producing Culture for the Digital Economy," *Social Text* 18, no. 2 (2000): 32.

25 Kücklich, "Precarious Playbour."

26   Dyer-Witheford and de Peuter, *Games of Empire*, 27.

27   Dyer-Witheford and de Peuter, *Games of Empire*, 50.

28   Ergin Bulut, "Glamor Above, Precarity Below: Immaterial Labor in the Video Game Industry," *Critical Studies in Media Communication* 32, no. 3 (2015): 203.

29   Bulut, "Glamor Above, Precarity Below," 203.

30   Ian G. Williams, "Crunched: Has the Games Industry Really Stopped Exploiting Its Workforce?," *Guardian*, February 18, 2015, www.theguardian.com/technology/2015/feb/18/crunched -games-industry-exploiting-workforce-ea-spouse-software.

31   Jennifer Pan, "Pink Collar," *Jacobin* 14 (2014), www.jacobinmag.com /2014/06/pink-collar/.

32   Pan, "Pink Collar."

33   Pan, "Pink Collar."

34   Pan, "Pink Collar."

35   Aphra Kerr and John D. Kelleher, "The Recruitment of Passion and Community in the Service of Capital: Community Managers in the Digital Games Industry," *Critical Studies in Media Communication* 32, no. 3 (2015): 190.

36   Kerr and Kelleher, "The Recruitment of Passion and Community," 190.

37   Kerr and Kelleher, "The Recruitment of Passion and Community," 190.

38   Kerr and Kelleher, "The Recruitment of Passion and Community," 191.

39   Dyer-Witheford and de Peuter, *Games of Empire*, 5.

40   Dyer-Witheford and de Peuter, *Games of Empire*, 77.

41   Pun Ngai, *Labour in China: Post-Socialist Transformations* (Cambridge, MA: Polity, 2016).

42   Bernard Girard, *The Google Way: How One Company Is Revolutionizing Management as We Know It* (San Francisco: No Starch Press, 2009).

43   Johanna Weststar, Victoria O'Meara, and Marie-Josée Legault, "Developer Satisfaction Survey 2017 Summary Report," International Game Developers Association, 2018, 22.

44   Weststar, O'Meara, and Legault, "Developer Satisfaction Survey 2017 Summary Report," 19.

45   Weststar, O'Meara, and Legault, "Developer Satisfaction Survey 2017 Summary Report," 32.

46   Dyer-Witheford and de Peuter, *Games of Empire*, 27.

47   Dyer-Witheford and de Peuter, *Games of Empire*, xxix.

48   Manuel Castells, *The Rise of the Network Society* (Oxford: Blackwell, 2000), 17.

49   Frederick W. Taylor, *The Principles of Scientific Management* (New York: Norton, 1967), 36.

50   Romano Alquati, *Sulla FIAT e altri scritti* (Milan: Feltrinelli, 1975), 51. Quoted in Devi Sacchetto, Emiliana Armano, and Steve Wright, "Coresearch and Counter-Research: Romano Alquati's Itinerary Within and Beyond Italian Radical Political Thought," *Viewpoint*, September 27,

2013, https://www.viewpointmag.com/2013/09/27/coresearch-and-counter-research-romano-alquatis-itinerary-within-and-beyond-italian-radical-political-thought.

51 Dyer-Witheford and de Peuter, *Games of Empire*, 27.

52 Dyer-Witheford and de Peuter, *Games of Empire*, 27.

53 Nathan Ensmenger and William Aspray, "Software as Labor Process," in *History of Computing: Software Issues – International Conference on the History of Computing*, eds. Ulf Hashagen, Reinhard Keil-Slawik, and Arthur L. Norberg (Paderborn, Germany: Heinz Nixdorf MuseumsForum, 2002), 157.

54 Ursula Huws, "Expression and Expropriation: The Dialectics of Autonomy and Control in Creative Labour," *Ephemera* 10, no. 3/4 (2010): 504.

55 Damian O'Doherty and Hugh Willmott, "The Decline of Labour Process Analysis and the Future Sociology of Work," *Sociology* 43, no. 5 (2009): 931–51.

56 Ensmenger and Aspray, "Software as Labor Process," 150.

57 Philip Kraft, *Programmers and Managers: The Routinization of Computer Programming in the United States* (New York: Springer-Verlag, 1977), 26.

58 Joan Greenbaum, "On Twenty-Five Years with Braverman's Labor and Monopoly Capital," *Monthly Review* 50, no. 8 (1999).

59 Graham Kirkpatrick, *Computer Games and the Social Imaginary* (Cambridge: Polity, 2013), 104.

60 Kirkpatrick, *Computer Games and the Social Imaginary*, 104.

61 Kirkpatrick, *Computer Games and the Social Imaginary*, 106.

62 Kirkpatrick, *Computer Games and the Social Imaginary*, 106.

63 Maxime Beaudoin, "Why I Quit My Dream Job at Ubisoft," Gingear Studio, January 21, 2016, http://gingearstudio.com/why-i-quit-my-dream-job-at-ubisoft.

64 Paul Thompson, Rachel Parker, and Stephen Cox, "Interrogating Creative Theory and Creative Work: Inside the Games Studio," *Sociology* 50, no. 2 (2015): 323.

65 Thompson, Parker, and Cox, "Interrogating Creative Theory," 342.

66 Christina Teipen, "Work and Employment in Creative Industries: The Video Games Industry: Germany, Sweden and Poland," *Economic and Industrial Democracy* 29, no. 3 (2008): 322.

67 Jean-François Gagné, "Inside vs Outside AAA," *A Blog About Games and Maybe Other Stuff*, January 26, 2016, https://jfgnord.wordpress.com/2016/01/26/inside-vs-outside-aaa/.

68 Thompson, Parker, and Cox, "Interrogating Creative Theory," 328.

69 Beaudoin, "Why I Quit my Dream Job at Ubisoft."

70 Jason Schreier, "The Messy, True Story behind the Making of Destiny," Kotaku, October 20, 2015, https://kotaku.com/the-messy-true-story-behind-the-making-of-destiny-1737556731.

71 Dyer-Witheford and de Peuter, *Games of Empire*, 59.

72   Jason Schreier, "Why Game Developers Keep Getting Laid Off," Kotaku,
      June 5, 2014, www.kotaku.co.uk/2014/06/05/game
      -developers-keep-getting-laid.

73   Anonymous programmer, quoted in Ian G. Williams, "Crunched.".

74   ea_spouse, "EA: The Human Story," *EA: The Human Story*, November 10,
      2004, https://ea-spouse.livejournal.com/274.html.

75   Williams, "Crunched."

76   International Game Developers Association, "Quality of Life in the
      Game Industry: Challenges and Best Practices," IGDA, 2004,
      www.igda.org.

77   Williams, "Crunched."

78   Ian Williams, "'You Can Sleep Here All Night': Video Games and Labor,"
      Jacobin, August 11, 2013, https://jacobinmag.com/2013/11
      /video-game-industry/.

79   Weststar, O'Meara, and Legault, "Developer Satisfaction Survey 2017
      Summary Report," 22.

80   Paul Tozour, "The Game Outcomes Project, Part 4: Crunch Makes Games
      Worse," *Gamasutra*, January 20, 2015, www.gamasutra.com/blogs
      /PaulTozour/20150120/234443/The_Game_Outcomes_Project_Part
      _4_Crunch_Makes_Games_Worse.php.

81   Marx, *Capital*.

82   Quoted in Jason Schreier, "The Horrible World of Video Game Crunch,"
      Kotaku, May 15, 2015, www.kotaku.co.uk/2015/05/15/crunch
      -time-game-developers-work-insane-hours.

83   Schreier, "The Horrible World of Video Game Crunch."

84   Williams, "Crunched."

85   Schreier, "The Horrible World of Video Game Crunch."

86   Dyer-Witheford and de Peuter, *Games of Empire*, 60.

87   *Notes from Below* editors, "The Workers' Inquiry and Social Composition."

88   Weststar, O'Meara, and Legault, "Developer Satisfaction Survey 2017
      Summary Report," 20.

89   Régis Renevey, "Creative Skillset Workforce Survey Breakdown," Ukie,
      May 20, 2015, http://ukie.org.uk/news/2015/05/creative
      -skillset-workforce-survey-breakdown.

90   Dan Pearson, "Survey: 45% of the UK Industry's Women Feel Gender Is
      a 'Barrier,'" GamesIndustry.biz, January 13, 2015, www.gamesindustry
      .biz/articles/2015-01-13-survey-45-percent-of-the-uk-industrys-women
      -feel-gender-is-a-barrier.

91   Lizzie Haines, "Why Are There So Few Women in Games?" (SlideShare
      presentation, Research for Media Training North West, Manchester, UK,
      September 2004), 13.

92   Dyer-Witheford and de Peuter, *Games of Empire*, 63.

93   Weststar, O'Meara, and Legault, "Developer Satisfaction Survey 2017
      Summary Report," 12.

94   Weststar, O'Meara, and Legault, "Developer Satisfaction Survey 2017 Summary Report," 17.

95   Weststar, O'Meara, and Legault, "Developer Satisfaction Survey 2017 Summary Report," 18.

96   Kirkpatrick, Computer Games and the Social Imaginary, 107.

97   Williams, "You Can Sleep Here All Night."

98   Kirkpatrick, *Computer Games and the Social Imaginary*, 108.

Organizing in the Videogames Industry

1   "Tech Workers Coalition," Tech Workers Coalition, 2018, https://techworkerscoalition.org.

2   R. K. Upadhya, "Disrupting Disruption: On Intervening against Technological Restructuring," *Notes from Below* 2 (March 30, 2018), www.notesfrombelow.org/article/disrupting-disruption.

3   Jason Prado, "Prospects for Organizing in the Tech Industry," *Notes from Below* 2 (March 30, 2018), www.notesfrombelow.org/article /prospects-for-organizing-the-tech-industry.

4   Tech Workers Coalition, "Tech Workers, Platform Workers, and Workers' Inquiry." *Notes from Below* 2 (March 30, 2018), www.notesfrombelow.org /article/tech-workers-platform-workers-and-workers-inquiry.

5   Tech Workers Coalition, "Tech Workers, Platform Workers, and Workers' Inquiry."

6   "Why We Strike," SAG-AFTRA, 2016, www.sagaftra.org/files /whywestrike.pdf.

7   Quoted in Ian Williams, "The Ongoing Voice Actor's Strike Is More than Just a Little Drama," *Waypoint*, December 29, 2016, https://waypoint.vice. com/en_us/article/nznyxq/the-ongoing-voice-actors-strike-is -more-than-just-a-little-drama.

8   Quoted in Williams, "The Ongoing Voice Actor's Strike."

9   Luke Plunkett, "The Video Game Voice-Actor's Strike Is Over," Kotaku, November 7, 2017, https://kotaku.com/the-video-game-voice -actors-strike-is-over-1820240476.

10   Dante Douglas, "Game Developers Need a Union," *Paste*, March 7, 2018, www.pastemagazine.com/articles/2018/03/game-developers-need-a -union.html.

11   Quoted in Ethan Gach, "Developers at One French Game Studio Have Been on Strike for a Month," Kotaku, March 16, 2018, https://kotaku .com/developers-at-one-french-game-studio-have-been-on-strik -1823833426.

12   This is a national collective bargaining agreement in France that mainly covers consulting firms.

13   Gach, "Developers at One French Game Studio."

14   Quoted in Gach, "Developers at One French Game Studio."

15   Gach, "Developers at One French Game Studio."

16   Quoted in Gach, "Developers at One French Game Studio."

17   "A Black and White Tri-Fold Leaflet," Game Workers Unite UK, 2018, http://gwu-uk.org/assets/trifold-bw-uk.pdf.

18   Matt Kim, "IGDA Director Says Capital, Not Unions, Will Keep Game Development Jobs Secure," US Gamer, January 19, 2018, www.usgamer .net/articles/igda-director-union-crunch-interview.

19   Ian Williams, "After Destroying Lives for Decades, Gaming Is Finally Talking Unionization," *Waypoint*, March 23, 2018, https://waypoint .vice.com/en_us/article/7xdv5e/after-destroying-lives-for-decades -gaming-is-finally-talking-unionization.

20   Williams, "After Destroying Lives for Decades."

21   Williams, "After Destroying Lives for Decades."

22   Williams, "After Destroying Lives for Decades."

23   Michelle Ehrhardt, "IGDA, Union-Busting and GDC 2018," *Unwinnable*, March 22, 2018, https://unwinnable.com/2018/03/22/igda-union -busting-and-gdc-2018.

24   Ehrhardt, "IGDA, Union-Busting and GDC 2018."

25   Game Workers Unite, "Game Workers Unite Zine," *Notes from Below* 2 (March 30, 2018), www.notesfrombelow.org/article/game-workers -unite-zine.

26   Game Workers Unite, "Game Workers Unite Zine."

27   Game Workers Unite, "Game Workers Unite Zine."

28   Quoted in Thomas Wilde, "'It's Very David and Goliath': Inside the Growing Effort to Unionize Video Game Developers," *Geekwire*, May 9, 2018, www.geekwire.com/2018/david-goliath-inside-growing-effort -unionize-video-game-developers.

29   Quoted in Wilde, "It's Very David and Goliath."

30   "Prospects for Organising the Videogames Industry: Interview with Game Workers Unite UK," interview by Jamie Woodcock, *Notes from Below* 3 (August 16, 2018), https://notesfrombelow.org/article /prospects-for-organising-the-videogames-industry.

31   "Prospects for Organising."

32   "Prospects for Organising."

33   "Prospects for Organising."

34   Jamie Woodcock, "Playing for Power," *Jacobin*, January 3, 2019, https:// jacobinmag.com/2019/01/video-game-workers-unite-union-uk.

35   See, for example, articles at https://notesfrombelow.org/.

Analyzing Culture

1   "Game Browser," MobyGames, last modified June 7, 2018, www.mobygames.com/browse/games/list-games/.

2   Dyer-Witheford and de Peuter, *Games of Empire*, xxix.

3   Ernest Mandel, *Delightful Murder: A Social History of the Crime Story* (Minneapolis: University of Minnesota Press, 1984), vi.

4   Mandel, *Delightful Murder*, viii.

5   Raymond Williams, *Television: Technology and Cultural Form* (London: Routledge, 1990), 1.

6   Williams, *Television*, 1.

7   Williams, *Television*, 122.

8   Karl Marx and Frederick Engels, *The German Ideology* (London: Lawrence and Wishart, 1970), 56.

9   Marx and Engels, *The German Ideology*, 47.

10 Karl Marx, *A Contribution to the Critique of Political Economy* (Progress Publishers: Moscow, 1977).

11 Terry Eagleton, *Marxism and Literary Criticism* (London: Routledge, 1989), xii–xiii.

12 Eagleton, *Marxism and Literary Criticism*, 2.

13 Eagleton, *Marxism and Literary Criticism*, 5.

14 Engels, letter to Joseph Bloch, 1890, quoted in Eagleton, *Marxism and Literary Criticism*, 9; italics in the original.

15 Eagleton, *Marxism and Literary Criticism*, 13.

16 Eagleton, *Marxism and Literary Criticism*, 13.

First-Person Shooters

1   Nina Huntemann, "The Problem with War Video Games," Kotaku, November 9, 2011, http://kotaku.com/5857878/the-problem-with-war -video-games.

2   Walter Benjamin, *The Work of Art in the Age of Mechanical Reproduction* (London: Penguin Books, 2008), 18.

3   Benjamin, *The Work of Art*, 9.

4   Maria Konnikova, "Why Gamers Can't Stop Playing First-Person Shooters," *New Yorker*, November 25, 2013, www.newyorker.com/tech /elements/why-gamers-cant-stop-playing-first-person-shooters.

5   Mihaly Csikszentmihalyi, *Flow: The Psychology of Optimal Experience* (New York: Harper Perennial, 1990).

6   Andrew Feenberg, "Alternative Modernity? Playing the Japanese Game of Culture," *Cultural Critique* 29 (1994): 107–38.

7   Mark R. Johnson and Jamie Woodcock, "Fighting Games and Go: Exploring the Aesthetics of Play in Professional Gaming," *Thesis Eleven* 138, no. 1 (2017): 32.

8   Konnikova, "Why Gamers Can't Stop Playing First-Person Shooters."

9   Michael Hitchens, "B.J.'s Family: A Survey of First Person Shooters and Their Avatars," in Proceedings of the Sixth Australasian Conference on Interactive Entertainment, ACM, 2009, p. 4.

10 Rune Klevjer, "Gladiator, Worker, Operative: The Hero of the First Person Shooter Adventure" (presentation, Level Up: Digital Games Research Conference, Utrecht University, Netherlands, 2003).

11 Hitchens, "B.J.'s Family."

12 Edge Staff, "The Making Of . . . Medal of Honor," *GamesRadar*, March 30, 2015, www.gamesradar.com/making-medal-honor/.

13 Edge Staff, "The Making Of . . . Medal of Honour."

14 James Orry, "Battlefield 1's Anthology Format Single Player Campaign Looks Amazing in First Trailer," *VideoGamer*, September 28, 2016,

www.videogamer.com/news/battlefield-1s-anthology-format-single
-player-campaign-looks-amazing-in-first-trailer.

15   Julie Muncy, "A First-Person Shooter Set in WWI Is Maaaybe Not the
      Best Idea," *Wired*, May 10, 2016, www.wired.com/2016/05
      /battlefield-1-wwi.

16   Wilfred Owen, *The Poems of Wilfred Owen* (Ware, UK: Wordsworth
      Editions, 1994), 60.

17   Adam Chapman, "It's Hard to Play in the Trenches: World War I,
      Collective Memory and Videogames," *Game Studies* 16, no. 2 (2016).

18   Quoted in "Call of Duty Q&A," GameSpot, May 1, 2003,
      www.gamespot.com/articles/call-of-duty-qanda/1100-6026083.

19   Owen Good, "Black Ops II Chooses Someone Who Failed the Call of
      Duty," Kotaku, May 4, 2012, http://kotaku.com/5907854
      /black-ops-2-chooses-someone-who-failed-the-call-of-duty.

20   Marianne Hirsch, *The Generation of Postmemory: Writing and Visual Culture*
      after the Holocaust (New York: Columbia University Press, 2008).

21   Adam Chapman, *Digital Games as History: How Videogames Represent the*
      Past and Offer Access to Historical Practice (New York: Routledge, 2016).

22   Kevin O'Neill and Bill Feenstra, "'Honestly, I Would Stick with
      the Books": Young Adults' Ideas about a Videogame as a Source of
      Historical Knowledge," *Game Studies* 16, no. 2 (2016).

23   "Exclusive: Inside the Making of Call of Duty 4," *Gamasutra*, March 11,
      2008, www.gamasutra.com/view/news/108762/Exclusive_Inside_The
      _Making_Of_Call_Of_Duty_4.php.

24   Steven Burns, "Death From Above: How COD4 Is the Most
      Realistic War Game Ever Made," *VideoGamer*, January 18, 2014,
      www.videogamer.com/features/death-from-above-how-cod4-is-the
      -most-realistic-war-game-ever-made.

25   Simon Parkin, "Call of Duty: Gaming's Role in the Military-Entertainment
      Complex," *Guardian*, October 22, 2014, www.theguardian.com
      /technology/2014/oct/22/call-of-duty-gaming-role-military
      -entertainment-complex.

26   Good, "Black Ops II Chooses Someone Who Failed."

27   Stephen Totilo, "Call of Duty Creators Say Oliver North Helped Make
      Their Game More Authentic," Kotaku, May 24, 2012, http://kotaku.com
      /5913092/call-of-duty-makers-say-controversial-oliver-north-helped
      -make-their-game-more-authentic.

28   Benedict Anderson, *Imagined Communities* (London: Verso, 1983).

29   Matthew T. Payne, *Playing War: Military Video Games after 9/11* (New
      York: NYU Press, 2016), 7–8.

30   Payne, *Playing War*, 5.

31   Tom Bissell, "Thirteen Ways of Looking at a Shooter," *Grantland*, July
      12, 2012, http://grantland.com/features/line-explores-reasons
      -why-play-shooter-games.

32 Kristine Jørgensen, "The Positive Discomfort of Spec Ops: The Line," *Game Studies* 16, no. 2 (2016).

33 Jørgensen, "The Positive Discomfort of Spec Ops."

34 Jørgensen, "The Positive Discomfort of Spec Ops."

35 Daniel Joseph, "A Line in a Cyclone," *First Person Scholar*, December 21, 2016, www.firstpersonscholar.com/a-line-in-a-cyclone.

36 Bissell, "Thirteen Ways of Looking at a Shooter."

Role-Playing, Simulations, and Strategy

1 Roger Caillois, *Man, Play and Games* (Urbana and Chicago: University of Illinois Press, 2001), 12.

2 Patricia Hernandez, "There's No Such Thing as a Game without Politics or an Agenda," Kotaku, August 30, 2012, https://kotaku.com/5939367 /theres-no-such-thing-as-a-game-without-politics-or-an-agenda.

3 National Museum of Play, "2016 World Video Game Hall of Fame Inductees Announced," 2016, www.museumofplay.org/press/releases /2016/05/2688-2016-world-video-game-hall-fame-inductees-announced.

4 Quoted in National Museum of Play, "2016 World Video Game Hall of Fame."

5 Quoted in Charlie Brooker, "How Videogames Changed the World," Channel 4, November 30, 2013.

6 Quoted in Alexa Ray Corriea, "Death and Pool Ladders in The Sims 4," *Polygon*, October 9, 2014, www.polygon.com/2014/10/9/6951277 /death-and-pool-ladders-in-the-sims-4.

7 Hernandez, "There's No Such Thing."

8 Quoted in Jason Schreier, "Sid Meier: The Father of Civilization," Kotaku, June 26, 2013, https://kotaku.com/the-father-of-civilization -584568276.

9 Schreier, "Sid Meier."

10 Quoted in Schreier, "Sid Meier."

11 Eric Williams, *Capitalism and Slavery* (Chapel Hill and London: University of North Carolina Press, 1994).

12 Chris Suellentrop, "'Civilization' Creator Sid Meier: 'I Didn't Really Expect to Be a Game Designer,'" *Rolling Stone*, May 8, 2017.

13 Quoted in Suellentrop, "'Civilization' Creator Sid Meier."

14 Quoted in Schreier, "Sid Meier."

15 Colin Campbell, "Karl Marx and the Historical Determinism of Video Games," *Polygon*, March 18, 2018, www.polygon.com/platform/ amp/2016/3/18/11264172/karl-marx-and-the-historical -determinism-of-video-games.

16 Kevin Schut, "Strategic Simulations and Our Past: The Bias of Computer Games in the Presentation of History," *Games and Culture* 2, no. 3 (2007): 221.

17 Hal Draper, "The Two Souls of Socialism," *New Politics*, 5, no. 1 (1966): 58; italics in the original.

18   Quoted in Bryant Francis, "Firaxis Partners with Glasslab for Educational Version of Civilization V," *Gamasutra*, June 23, 2016, www.gamasutra.com/view/news/275717/Firaxis_partners_with _GlassLab_for_educational_version_of_Civilization_V.php.

19   Marx and Engels, *The German Ideology*, 60.

20   Suellentrop, "'Civilization' Creator Sid Meier."

Political Videogames

1   Woodcock, *Working the Phones*.

2   Patricia Hernandez, "There's No Such Thing as a Game without Politics or an Agenda," Kotaku, August 30, 2012, https://kotaku.com/5939367 /theres-no-such-thing-as-a-game-without-politics-or-an-agenda.

3   Quoted in Chris Baraniuk, "Video Games Become Political as US Election Looms," *New Scientist*, October 28, 2016, www.newscientist .com/article/2110736-video-games-become-political-as-us-election-looms.

4   Bertell Ollman, "Ballbuster? True Confessions of a Marxist Businessman," in *Dialectical Marxism: The Writings of Bertell Ollman*, www.nyu.edu/projects/ollman/docs/bb_ch01.php.

5   Ollman, "Ballbuster?"

6   Ollman, "Ballbuster?"

7   Quoted in Ollman, "Ballbuster?"

8   Quoted in Ollman, "Ballbuster?"

9   Caillois, *Man, Play and Games*, 13.

10   Ollman, "Ballbuster?"

11   Keith Plocek, "Most Popular Marxist Board Game," *Mental Floss*, August 12, 2014, http://mentalfloss.com/article/58318/story-class -struggle-americas-most-popular-marxist-board-game.

12   Quoted in Plocek, "Most Popular Marxist Board Game."

13   Molleindustria, "Phone Story," Phone Story, 2011, www.phonestory.org.

14   Stuart Dredge, "Apple Bans Satirical iPhone Game Phone Story from Its App Store," *Guardian*, September 14, 2011, www.theguardian.com /technology/appsblog/2011/sep/14/apple-phone-story-rejection.

15   Molleindustria, "Phone Story."

16   Dredge, "Apple Bans Satirical iPhone Game."

17   Molleindustria, "To Build a Better Mousetrap," 2014, http://www .molleindustria.org/to-build-a-better-mousetrap.

18   Joseph Bernstein, "The New Marxism Comes to Computer Games," *BuzzFeed*, May 5, 2014, www.buzzfeed.com/josephbernstein/the-new -marxism-comes-to-computer-games.

19   David Leblanc, "Working at Play: Alienation, Refusal, and Every Day the Same Dream," *First Person Scholar*, December 14, 2016, www.firstpersonscholar.com/working-at-play.

20   Quoted in Leblanc, "Working at Play."

21   Leblanc, "Working at Play."

22   John Walker, "Wot I Think: Papers, Please," *Rock Paper Shotgun*, August 12, 2013, www.rockpapershotgun.com/2013/08/12/ wot-i-think-papers-please.

23   Walker, "Wot I Think: Papers, Please."

24   Keith Stuart, "War Games – Developers Find New Ways to Explore Military Conflict," *Guardian*, July 15, 2014, www.theguardian.com /technology/2014/jul/15/war-games-developers-military-conflict.

25   Marijam Didžgalvytė, "The Uber Game Shows the Latent Power of Political Video Games," Kotaku, February 8, 2018, www.kotaku.co .uk/2018/02/08/the-uber-game-shows-the-latent-power-of -political-video-games.

26   Didžgalvytė, "The Uber Game Shows the Latent Power."

27   Marijam Didžgalvytė, "'Corbyn Run' Highlights the Stakes of This Week's British Election," *Waypoint*, June 6, 2017, https://waypoint.vice .com/en_us/article/a3zvpp/corbyn-run-highlights-the-stakes-of -this-weeks-british-election.

28   Quoted in Didžgalvytė, "'Corbyn Run' Highlights the Stakes."

29   ·Didžgalvytė, "'Corbyn Run' Highlights the Stakes."

30   Didžgalvytė, "The Uber Game Shows the Latent Power."

31   *The Supergamers*, directed by Chris Boulding, London: BBC, 2016.

32   Mark R. Johnson and Jamie Woodcock. "It's Like the Gold Rush: The Lives and Careers of Professional Video Game Streamers on Twitch.tv," Information, *Communication and Society* 22, no. 3 (2017): 336–51.

33   Jason Schreier, "Sid Meier: The Father of Civilization," Kotaku, June 26, 2013, https://kotaku.com/the-father-of-civilization-584568276.

34   Dyer-Witheford and de Peuter, *Games of Empire*, 28.

35   Katie Sola, "'Pokémon GO' Poll Shows 69% of Users Play at Work," *Forbes*, July 19, 2016.

36   David Graeber, *Bullshit Jobs: A Theory* (London: Penguin, 2018).

37   Quoted in Quoctrung Bui, "Why Some Men Don't Work: Video Games Have Gotten Really Good," *New York Times*, July 3, 2017, www.nytimes .com/2017/07/03/upshot/why-some-men-dont-work-video-games-have -gotten-really-good.html.

38   Bui, "Why Some Men Don't Work."

39   Johan Huizinga, *Homo Ludens: A Study of the Play-Element in Culture* (Kettering, OH: Angelico Press, 2006), 12.

Online Play

1   Lars Kristensen and Ulf Wilhelmsson, "Roger Caillois and Marxism: A Game Studies Perspective," *Games and Culture* 12, no. 4 (2017): 389.

2   Paul Tassi, "Riot Games Reveals 'League of Legends' Has 100 Million Monthly Players," *Forbes*, September 13, 2016, www.forbes.com/sites /insertcoin/2016/09/13/riot-games-reveals-league-of-legends-has-100 -million-monthly-players/#322ab3b55aa8.

3   Caillois, *Man, Play and Games*, 13.

4   Dyer-Witheford and de Peuter, *Games of Empire*, 18.

5   Quoted in Tracey Lien, "No Girls Allowed," *Polygon*, December 2, 2013, www.polygon.com/features/2013/12/2/5143856/no-girls-allowed.

6   Lien, "No Girls Allowed."

7   Quoted in Lien, "No Girls Allowed."

8   Lien, "No Girls Allowed."

9   James D. Ivory, "Still a Man's Game: Gender Representation in Online Reviews of Video Games," *Mass Communication and Society* 9, no. 1 (2006): 111.

10   Monica K. Miller and Alicia Summers, "Gender Differences in Video Game Characters' Roles, Appearances, and Attire as Portrayed in Video Game Magazines," *Sex Roles* 57 (2007): 740.

11   Kaitlin Tremblay, "Intro to Gender Criticism for Gamers: From Princess Peach, to Claire Redfield, to FemSheps," *Gamasutra*, June 1, 2012, www.gamasutra.com/blogs/KaitlinTremblay/20120601/171613/Intro _to_Gender_Criticism_for_Gamers_From_Princess_Peach_to_Claire _Redfield_to_FemSheps.php?print=1.

12   Tremblay, "Intro to Gender Criticism for Gamers."

13   Lien, "No Girls Allowed."

14   Torill Elvira Mortensen, "Anger, Fear, and Games: The Long Event of #GamerGate," *Games and Culture* 13, no. 8 (2016): 787 806.

15   Paulo Ruffino, "Parasites to Gaming: Learning from GamerGate" (paper, Proceedings of 1st International Joint Conference of DiGRA and FDG, Dundee, UK, 2016).

16   Cherie Todd, "Commentary: GamerGate and Resistance to the Diversification of Gaming Culture," *Women's Studies Journal* 29, no. 1 (2015): 64.

17   Mortensen, "Anger, Fear, and Games," 14.

18   Jake Swearingen, "Steve Bannon Saw the 'Monster Power' of Angry Gamers While Farming Gold in World of Warcraft," *New York*, July 18, 2017, http://nymag.com/intelligencer/2017/07/steve-bannon-world -of-warcraft-gold-farming.html.

19   Joshua Green, *Devil's Bargain: Steve Bannon, Donald Trump, and the Storming of the Presidency* (New York: Penguin, 2017), 81.

20   Angela Nagle, *Kill All Normies: Online Culture Wars from 4chan and Tumblr to Trump and the Alt-Right* (Winchester: Zero Books, 2017); Matt Lees, "What Gamergate Should Have Taught Us about the 'Alt-Right,'" *Guardian*, December 1, 2016, www.theguardian.com/technology/2016 /dec/01/gamergate-alt-right-hate-trump.

21   Robert Purchese, "ArenaNet Fires Two Guild Wars 2 Writers over Twitter Exchange with YouTuber," *Eurogamer*, July 7, 2018, www .eurogamer.net/articles/2018-07-06-arenanet-fires-two-guild-wars -2-writers-over-twitter-exchange-with-youtuber.

22   Quoted in Keith Stuart, "Richard Bartle: We Invented Multiplayer Games as a Political Gesture," *Guardian*, November 17, 2014, www

.theguardian.com/technology/2014/nov/17/richard-bartle-multiplayer
-games-political-gesture.

Conclusion

1   Dyer-Witheford and de Peuter, *Games of Empire*, 66.

2   Ian Williams, "'You Can Sleep Here All Night': Video Games and Labor,"
     Jacobin, August 11, 2013, https://jacobinmag.com/2013/11/video
     -game-industry/.

3   *Notes from Below* editors, "The Workers' Inquiry and Social Composition,"
     Notes from Below, issue 1, January 29, 2018, www
     .notesfrombelow.org/article/workers-inquiry-and-social-composition.

4   Dyer-Witheford and de Peuter, *Games of Empire*, 229.

5   Dyer-Witheford and de Peuter, *Games of Empire*, 228.

6   Bertell Ollman, "Ballbuster?"

7   Benjamin, *The Work of Art in the Age of Mechanical Reproduction*, 38.

8   Stuart Hall, "Notes on Deconstructing the Popular," in *People's History
     and Socialist Theory*, ed. Raphael Samuel (London: Routledge & Kegan
     Paul, 1981), 239.

9   Matt Lees, "What Gamergate Should Have Taught Us about the
     'Alt-Right,'" *Guardian*, December 1, 2016, www.theguardian.com/
     technology/2016/dec/01/gamergate-alt-right-hate-trump.

10   Leigh Alexander, "'Gamers' Don't Have to Be Your Audience. 'Gamers'
     Are Over," *Gamastura*, August 28, 2014, www.gamasutra.com/view
     /news/224400/Gamers_dont_have_to_be_your_audience_Gamers
     _are_over.php.

11   Karl Marx, "A Workers' Inquiry," *New International* 4, no. 12 (1938): 379.

Index

ABOUT THE AUTHOR

Dr Jamie Woodcock is a researcher at the Oxford Internet Institute, University of Oxford. He is the author of *Working The Phones*, a study of a call center in the UK inspired by the workers' inquiry. His research focuses on labor, work, the gig economy, platforms, resistance, organizing, and videogames. Jamie is on the editorial board of *Notes from Below* and *Historical Materialism*.

ABOUT HAYMARKET BOOKS

Haymarket Books is a radical, independent, nonprofit book publisher based in Chicago. Our mission is to publish books that contribute to struggles for social and economic justice. We strive to make our books a vibrant and organic part of social movements and the education and development of a critical, engaged, international left.

We take inspiration and courage from our namesakes, the Haymarket martyrs, who gave their lives fighting for a better world. Their 1886 struggle for the eight-hour day—which gave us May Day, the international workers' holiday—reminds workers around the world that ordinary people can organize and struggle for their own liberation. These struggles continue today across the globe—struggles against oppression, exploitation, poverty, and war.

Since our founding in 2001, Haymarket Books has published more than five hundred titles. Radically independent, we seek to drive a wedge into the risk-averse world of corporate book publishing. Our authors include Noam Chomsky, Arundhati Roy, Rebecca Solnit, Angela Y. Davis, Howard Zinn, Amy Goodman, Wallace Shawn, Mike Davis, Winona LaDuke, Ilan Pappé, Richard Wolff, Dave Zirin, Keeanga-Yamahtta Taylor, Nick Turse, Dahr Jamail, David Barsamian, Elizabeth Laird, Amira Hass, Mark Steel, Avi Lewis, Naomi Klein, and Neil Davidson. We are also the trade publishers of the acclaimed Historical Materialism Book Series and of Dispatch Books.